THE
HOME OWNER'S
JOURNAL

ALSO BY CONFLUENCE BOOKS:

Murdock's Auto Service Journal

Track Auto Maintenance, Repairs, Upgrades, Miles-Per-Gallon

THE HOME OWNER'S JOURNAL

What I Did
and
When I Did It

FIFTH EDITION

BY COLLEEN JENKINS

Confluence
Books

THE HOME OWNER'S JOURNAL

What I Did and When I Did It

• FIFTH EDITION •

Published by:

CONFLUENCE BOOKS
2232 North 7th Street, Suite 15
Grand Junction, CO 81501
(970) 257-0606
(800) 444-5450
www.ConfluenceBooks.com

The Home Owner's Journal is available at discount
when purchased in bulk quantities.

ISBN 0-9725591-1-6

65th printing

CONTENTS

Contents *(continued)*

FOREWORD

Colleen Jenkins, who wrote the original edition of *The Home Owner's Journal* back in 1986, said, "This is the book I needed when we first bought our home forty years ago. I don't know how I managed without it."

In fact, most of us do not manage well at all. We make many mistakes involving, say, wallpapering the bathroom or painting the outside of the house. The consequence of our failure, for example, to record how much paint we previously used can be two gallons of custom mixed, non-returnable, hazardous-waste paint! Other consequences can be extra carpet, lost warranties, or the inability to match a cabinet stain because we didn't record it initially. We hope this book offers a solution to those consequences. Many users apparently feel that it does: Over 1/2 million copies of *The Home Owner's Journal* have been sold.

Colleen thought that writing this book would be simple, but she subsequently wrote many drafts before arriving at what we believe is a very practical, easy-to-use and flexible journal. Since all homes are different, there are, no doubt, various sections of this book that will not apply to you. Complete only those sections that apply. We suggest making all entries in pencil to allow for easy corrections and updates.

The book has evolved over the years. This Fifth Edition, which you hold in your hand, incorporates many comments that we have received from users. We have added a "Notes" column on the outer edge of each page, which resulted in our adding an inch to the width of this edition. This is because many users told us the book needed more space for notes and plans. Users also requested changes in the organization of the book. Accordingly, we have chosen a more consistent terminology and arrangement throughout.

We suspect that users of the book frequently read various tips and instructions having to do with home repair and remodeling. As such, we've added our own "Tips" and "How To's", as well as some amusing witticisms. You will see these at the lower corner of each right hand page.

We hope that you will let us know what you think of the book, and that you'll offer suggestions and changes to improve it even more. Please call us at 800-444-5450, or log on to *ConfluenceBooks.com.*

LIVING ROOM

FLOOR COVERING

MEASUREMENTS • Floor

Width _____ X Depth _____ = _____ sq. ft.

TYPE & MATERIAL • Floor Covering

Description *(nylon carpet, ceramic tile, etc.)* _____
Brand & pattern _____
Color & number _____
Backing type _____ Pad type _____

PURCHASE • Floor Covering

Retailer _____
Date _____ Cost/unit $ _____
No. of units _____ Total cost $ _____
Warranty _____

INSTALLATION • Floor Covering

Installer _____
Date _____ Cost $ _____

CLEANING & REFINISHING • Floor Covering

Company _____
Date _____ Cost $ _____
Company _____
Date _____ Cost $ _____

CEILING COVERING

TYPE & MATERIAL • Ceiling Covering

Description *(paint, spray texture, etc.)* _____
Brand & pattern _____
Color & number _____

PURCHASE • Ceiling Covering

Retailer _____
Date _____ Cost/unit $ _____
No. of units _____ Total cost $ _____
Warranty _____

INSTALLATION • Ceiling Covering

Installer _____
Date _____ Cost $ _____

Notes

_____
_____
_____
_____
_____
_____
_____
_____
_____
_____
_____
_____
_____
_____
_____
_____

A mediocre idea that generates enthusiasm will go further than a great idea that inspires no one.

—Mary Kay Ash

_____
_____
_____

1

_____

LIVING ROOM

Notes

WALL COVERING

MEASUREMENTS • Walls

North: Width _____ X Height _____ = _____ sq. ft.

South: Width _____ X Height _____ = _____ sq. ft.

East: Width _____ X Height _____ = _____ sq. ft.

West: Width _____ X Height _____ = _____ sq. ft.

▶ **TYPE & MATERIAL** • First Wall Covering

Description _(paint, paper, paneling, etc.)_ _____

Brand & pattern _____

Color & number _____

PURCHASE • First Wall Covering

Retailer _____

Date _____ Cost/unit $ _____

No. of units _____ Total cost $ _____

Warranty _____

INSTALLATION • First Wall Covering

Installer _____

Date _____ Cost $ _____

CLEANING & REFINISHING • First Wall Covering

Company _____

  Date _____ Cost $ _____

Company _____

  Date _____ Cost $ _____

▶ **TYPE & MATERIAL** • Second Wall Covering

Description _(paint, paper, paneling, etc.)_ _____

Brand & pattern _____

Color & number _____

PURCHASE • Second Wall Covering

Retailer _____

Date _____ Cost/unit $ _____

No. of units _____ Total cost $ _____

Warranty _____

INSTALLATION • Second Wall Covering

Installer _____

Date _____ Cost $ _____

CLEANING & REFINISHING • Second Wall Covering

Company _____

  Date _____ Cost $ _____

Company _____

  Date _____ Cost $ _____

WINDOWS

MEASUREMENTS • Windows

Window 1: Width _____ Height _____
Window 2: Width _____ Height _____
Window 3: Width _____ Height _____

TYPE & MATERIAL • Windows

Description *(vinyl casement, etc.)* _____
Brand & model _____

PURCHASE • Windows

Retailer _____
Date _____ Cost/unit $ _____
No. of units _____ Total cost $ _____
Warranty _____

INSTALLATION • Windows

Installer _____
Date _____ Cost $ _____

WINDOW TREATMENTS

MEASUREMENTS • Window Treatments

Treatment 1: Width _____ X Height _____ = _____ sq. ft.
Treatment 2: Width _____ X Height _____ = _____ sq. ft.
Treatment 3: Width _____ X Height _____ = _____ sq. ft.

TYPE & MATERIAL • Window Treatments

Description *(draperies, blinds, etc.)* _____
    Brand & model _____
    Color & number _____
Description *(draperies, blinds, etc.)* _____
    Brand & model _____
    Color & number _____

PURCHASE • Window Treatments

Retailer _____
Date _____ Cost/unit $ _____
No. of units _____ Total cost $ _____
Warranty _____

INSTALLATION • Window Treatments

Installer _____
Date _____ Cost $ _____

CLEANING & REFINISHING • Window Treatments

Company _____
    Date _____ Cost $ _____

LIVING ROOM

Notes

_____
_____
_____
_____
_____
_____
_____
_____
_____
_____
_____
_____
_____
_____
_____
_____
_____
_____
_____
_____

Tip: If you need help in visualizing paint colors in a room, you can buy a small amount of the color you like and paint a poster board. Then you can move the board around to different walls to see how the paint will look at different times of the day, and in different lighting.

3

LIVING ROOM

✏️ *Notes*

_____
_____
_____
_____
_____
_____
_____
_____
_____
_____
_____
_____
_____
_____
_____
_____
_____
_____
_____
_____
_____
_____
_____
_____
_____

DOORS

MEASUREMENTS • Doors

First Door: Second Door:
Width _____ Height _____   Width _____ Height _____

▶ **TYPE & MATERIAL** • First Door
Description *(oak, masonite, etc.)* _____
Brand & style _____
Color & number _____
Hardware description _____

PURCHASE • First Door
Retailer _____
Date _____   Cost/unit $ _____
No. of units _____   Total cost $ _____
Warranty _____

INSTALLATION • First Door
Installer _____
Date _____   Cost $ _____

CLEANING & REFINISHING • First Door
Company _____
  Date _____   Cost $ _____
Company _____
  Date _____   Cost $ _____

▶ **TYPE & MATERIAL** • Second Door
Description *(oak, masonite, etc.)* _____
Brand & style _____
Color & number _____
Hardware description _____

PURCHASE • Second Door
Retailer _____
Date _____   Cost/unit $ _____
No. of units _____   Total cost $ _____
Warranty _____

INSTALLATION • Second Door
Installer _____
Date _____   Cost $ _____

CLEANING & REFINISHING • Second Door
Company _____
  Date _____   Cost $ _____
Company _____
  Date _____   Cost $ _____

SAMPLES

Attach Swatch or Daub Paint Here

CLOSETS

DIAGRAMS/EXTRA NOTES

Notes

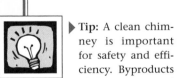

Tip: A clean chimney is important for safety and efficiency. Byproducts of burning wood build up in your chimney or flue pipe and are highly combustible. Have a qualified professional inspect and/or clean your chimney often.

KITCHEN

Notes

_____
_____
_____
_____
_____
_____
_____
_____
_____
_____
_____
_____
_____
_____
_____
_____
_____
_____
_____
_____
_____
_____
_____
_____
_____
_____
_____
_____
_____

_____

FLOOR COVERING

MEASUREMENTS • Floor
   Width _____ X Depth _____ = _____ sq. ft.

TYPE & MATERIAL • Floor Covering
   Description *(nylon carpet, ceramic tile, etc.)* _____
   Brand & pattern _____
   Color & number _____
   Backing type _____ Pad type _____

PURCHASE • Floor Covering
   Retailer _____
   Date _____ Cost/unit $ _____
   No. of units _____ Total cost $ _____
   Warranty _____

INSTALLATION • Floor Covering
   Installer _____
   Date _____ Cost $ _____

CLEANING & REFINISHING • Floor Covering
   Company _____
      Date _____ Cost $ _____
   Company _____
      Date _____ Cost $ _____

CEILING COVERING

TYPE & MATERIAL • Ceiling Covering
   Description *(paint, spray texture, etc.)* _____
   Brand & pattern _____
   Color & number _____

PURCHASE • Ceiling Covering
   Retailer _____
   Date _____ Cost/unit $ _____
   No. of units _____ Total cost $ _____
   Warranty _____

INSTALLATION • Ceiling Covering
   Installer _____
   Date _____ Cost $ _____

WALL COVERING

MEASUREMENTS • Walls

North: Width _____ X Height _____ = _____ sq. ft.
South: Width _____ X Height _____ = _____ sq. ft.
East: Width _____ X Height _____ = _____ sq. ft.
West: Width _____ X Height _____ = _____ sq. ft.

▶ **TYPE & MATERIAL** • First Wall Covering

Description *(paint, paper, paneling, etc.)* _____
Brand & pattern _____
Color & number _____

PURCHASE • First Wall Covering

Retailer _____
Date _____ Cost/unit $ _____
No. of units _____ Total cost $ _____
Warranty _____

INSTALLATION • First Wall Covering

Installer _____
Date _____ Cost $ _____

CLEANING & REFINISHING • First Wall Covering

Company _____
  Date _____ Cost $ _____
Company _____
  Date _____ Cost $ _____

▶ **TYPE & MATERIAL** • Second Wall Covering

Description *(paint, paper, paneling, etc.)* _____
Brand & pattern _____
Color & number _____

PURCHASE • Second Wall Covering

Retailer _____
Date _____ Cost/unit $ _____
No. of units _____ Total cost $ _____
Warranty _____

INSTALLATION • Second Wall Covering

Installer _____
Date _____ Cost $ _____

CLEANING & REFINISHING • Second Wall Covering

Company _____
  Date _____ Cost $ _____
Company _____
  Date _____ Cost $ _____

Notes

The room within is the great fact about the building.

—Frank Lloyd Wright

7

KITCHEN

Notes

_____
_____
_____
_____
_____
_____
_____
_____
_____
_____
_____
_____
_____
_____
_____
_____
_____
_____
_____
_____
_____
_____
_____
_____
_____
_____
_____

WINDOWS

MEASUREMENTS • Windows

Window 1: Width _____ Height _____
Window 2: Width _____ Height _____
Window 3: Width _____ Height _____

TYPE & MATERIAL • Windows

Description *(vinyl casement, etc.)* _____
Brand & model _____

PURCHASE • Windows

Retailer _____
Date _____ Cost/unit $ _____
No. of units _____ Total cost $ _____
Warranty _____

INSTALLATION • Windows

Installer _____
Date _____ Cost $ _____

WINDOW TREATMENTS

MEASUREMENTS • Window Treatments

Treatment 1: Width _____ X Height _____ = _____ sq. ft.
Treatment 2: Width _____ X Height _____ = _____ sq. ft.
Treatment 3: Width _____ X Height _____ = _____ sq. ft.

TYPE & MATERIAL • Window Treatments

Description *(draperies, blinds, etc.)* _____
  Brand & model _____
  Color & number _____
Description *(draperies, blinds, etc.)* _____
  Brand & model _____
  Color & number _____

PURCHASE • Window Treatments

Retailer _____
Date _____ Cost/unit $ _____
No. of units _____ Total cost $ _____
Warranty _____

INSTALLATION • Window Treatments

Installer _____
Date _____ Cost $ _____

CLEANING & REFINISHING • Window Treatments

Company _____
  Date _____ Cost $ _____

DOOR

MEASUREMENTS • Door
Width _____ Height _____

TYPE & MATERIAL • Door
Description *(oak, masonite, etc.)* _____
Brand & style _____
Color & number _____
Hardware description _____

PURCHASE • Door
Retailer _____
Date _____ Cost/unit $ _____
No. of units _____ Total cost $ _____
Warranty _____

INSTALLATION • Door
Installer _____
Date _____ Cost $ _____

CLEANING & REFINISHING • Door
Company _____
Date _____ Cost $ _____
Company _____

CABINETS

TYPE & MATERIAL • Cabinets
Material *(oak, steel, etc.)* _____
Brand & style _____
Stain/paint color & number _____

PURCHASE • Cabinets
Retailer _____
Date _____ Cost $ _____
Warranty _____

INSTALLATION • Cabinets
Installer _____
Date _____ Cost $ _____

CLEANING & REFINISHING • Cabinets
Company _____
Date _____ Cost $ _____
Company _____
Date _____ Cost $ _____

Notes

HOW TO

MEASURE A WINDOW

For draperies, rods should be mounted 4 inches above the glass to conceal the pleats. Determine the length of rod by measuring the width of the window glass and adding the *stack back*,* which is usually 1/3 the width of window glass on each side.

*The room it takes for drapes to clear the window when open.

9

KITCHEN

Notes

COUNTERTOPS

TYPE & MATERIAL • Countertops
Material *(formica, tile, granite, etc.)*
Brand & pattern
Color & number

PURCHASE • Countertops
Retailer
Date _____ Cost $ _____
Warranty

INSTALLATION • Countertops
Installer
Date _____ Cost $ _____

CLEANING & REFINISHING • Countertops
Company
Date _____ Cost $ _____
Company
Date _____ Cost $ _____
Company
Date _____ Cost $ _____

APPLIANCES

Type *(range, dishwasher, etc.)*
Manufacturer
Model/Lot no. _____ Serial no. _____
Retailer
Date _____ Cost $ _____ Warranty period _____
Authorized service center
Maintenance/service

Type *(range, dishwasher, etc.)*
Manufacturer
Model/Lot no. _____ Serial no. _____
Retailer
Date _____ Cost $ _____ Warranty period _____
Authorized service center
Maintenance/service

Appliances *(continued)*

Type *(range, dishwasher, etc.)* _____
Manufacturer _____
Model/Lot no. _____ Serial no. _____
Retailer _____
Date _____ Cost $ _____ Warranty period _____
Authorized service center _____
Maintenance/service _____
_____

Type *(range, dishwasher, etc.)* _____
Manufacturer _____
Model/Lot no. _____ Serial no. _____
Retailer _____
Date _____ Cost $ _____ Warranty period _____
Authorized service center _____
Maintenance/service _____
_____

Type *(range, dishwasher, etc.)* _____
Manufacturer _____
Model/Lot no. _____ Serial no. _____
Retailer _____
Date _____ Cost $ _____ Warranty period _____
Authorized service center _____
Maintenance/service _____
_____

SAMPLES

Attach Swatch or Daub Paint Here

Notes
_____
_____
_____
_____
_____
_____
_____
_____
_____
_____
_____
_____
_____
_____
_____
_____
_____

Tip: When working on your remodeling budget, save money by planning ahead! Choose everything you want to do to the room to help define your budget. It is wise to save 10 to 20 percent of your budget for those last minute details!

KITCHEN

Notes

FIXTURES

PANTRY/CLOSET

DIAGRAMS/EXTRA NOTES

DINING ROOM

FLOOR COVERING

MEASUREMENTS • Floor
Width _____ X Depth _____ = _____ sq. ft.

TYPE & MATERIAL • Floor Covering
Description *(nylon carpet, ceramic tile, etc.)* _____
Brand & pattern _____
Color & number _____
Backing type _____ Pad type _____

PURCHASE • Floor Covering
Retailer _____
Date _____ Cost/unit $ _____
No. of units _____ Total cost $ _____
Warranty _____

INSTALLATION • Floor Covering
Installer _____
Date _____ Cost $ _____

CLEANING & REFINISHING • Floor Covering
Company _____
    Date _____ Cost $ _____
Company _____
    Date _____ Cost $ _____

CEILING COVERING

TYPE & MATERIAL • Ceiling Covering
Description *(paint, spray texture, etc.)* _____
Brand & pattern _____
Color & number _____

PURCHASE • Ceiling Covering
Retailer _____
Date _____ Cost/unit $ _____
No. of units _____ Total cost $ _____
Warranty _____

INSTALLATION • Ceiling Covering
Installer _____
Date _____ Cost $ _____

Notes
_____
_____
_____
_____
_____
_____
_____
_____
_____
_____
_____
_____
_____
_____

No matter under what circumstances you leave it, home does not cease to be home. No matter how you lived there— well or poorly.

—Joseph Brodsky,
on leaving the USSR

_____
_____
_____

13

DINING ROOM

Notes

_____
_____
_____
_____
_____
_____
_____
_____
_____
_____
_____
_____
_____
_____
_____
_____
_____
_____
_____
_____
_____
_____
_____
_____
_____
_____
_____
_____
_____
_____
_____
_____

WALL COVERING

MEASUREMENTS • Walls

North: Width _____ X Height _____ = _____ sq. ft.
South: Width _____ X Height _____ = _____ sq. ft.
East: Width _____ X Height _____ = _____ sq. ft.
West: Width _____ X Height _____ = _____ sq. ft.

▶ **TYPE & MATERIAL** • First Wall Covering
Description _(paint, paper, paneling, etc.)_ _____
Brand & pattern _____
Color & number _____

PURCHASE • First Wall Covering
Retailer _____
Date _____ Cost/unit $ _____
No. of units _____ Total cost $ _____
Warranty _____

INSTALLATION • First Wall Covering
Installer _____
Date _____ Cost $ _____

CLEANING & REFINISHING • First Wall Covering
Company _____
  Date _____ Cost $ _____
Company _____
  Date _____ Cost $ _____

▶ **TYPE & MATERIAL** • Second Wall Covering
Description _(paint, paper, paneling, etc.)_ _____
Brand & pattern _____
Color & number _____

PURCHASE • Second Wall Covering
Retailer _____
Date _____ Cost/unit $ _____
No. of units _____ Total cost $ _____
Warranty _____

INSTALLATION • Second Wall Covering
Installer _____
Date _____ Cost $ _____

CLEANING & REFINISHING • Second Wall Covering
Company _____
  Date _____ Cost $ _____
Company _____
  Date _____ Cost $ _____

WINDOWS

MEASUREMENTS • Windows

Window 1: Width _____ Height _____
Window 2: Width _____ Height _____
Window 3: Width _____ Height _____

TYPE & MATERIAL • Windows

Description *(vinyl casement, etc.)* _____
Brand & model _____

PURCHASE • Windows

Retailer _____
Date _____ Cost/unit $ _____
No. of units _____ Total cost $ _____
Warranty _____

INSTALLATION • Windows

Installer _____
Date _____ Cost $ _____

WINDOW TREATMENTS

MEASUREMENTS • Window Treatments

Treatment 1: Width _____ X Height _____ = _____ sq. ft.
Treatment 2: Width _____ X Height _____ = _____ sq. ft.
Treatment 3: Width _____ X Height _____ = _____ sq. ft.

TYPE & MATERIAL • Window Treatments

Description *(draperies, blinds, etc.)* _____
  Brand & model _____
  Color & number _____
Description *(draperies, blinds, etc.)* _____
  Brand & model _____
  Color & number _____

PURCHASE • Window Treatments

Retailer _____
Date _____ Cost/unit $ _____
No. of units _____ Total cost $ _____
Warranty _____

INSTALLATION • Window Treatments

Installer _____
Date _____ Cost $ _____

CLEANING & REFINISHING • Window Treatments

Company _____
  Date _____ Cost $ _____

Notes

Home is where the heart is and hence a moveable feast.

—Angela Carter,
(1940–1992)

DINING ROOM

DOORS

MEASUREMENTS • Doors

First Door: Second Door:

Width _____ Height _____   Width _____ Height _____

▶ **TYPE & MATERIAL** • First Door

Description *(oak, masonite, etc.)* _____

Brand & style _____

Color & number _____

Hardware description _____

PURCHASE • First Door

Retailer _____

Date _____ Cost/unit $ _____

No. of units _____ Total cost $ _____

Warranty _____

INSTALLATION • First Door

Installer _____

Date _____ Cost $ _____

CLEANING & REFINISHING • First Door

Company _____

Date _____ Cost $ _____

Company _____

Date _____ Cost $ _____

▶ **TYPE & MATERIAL** • Second Door

Description *(oak, masonite, etc.)* _____

Brand & style _____

Color & number _____

Hardware description _____

PURCHASE • Second Door

Retailer _____

Date _____ Cost/unit $ _____

No. of units _____ Total cost $ _____

Warranty _____

INSTALLATION • Second Door

Installer _____

Date _____ Cost $ _____

CLEANING & REFINISHING • Second Door

Company _____

Date _____ Cost $ _____

Company _____

Date _____ Cost $ _____

SAMPLES

Attach Swatch or Daub Paint Here

CLOSETS

DIAGRAMS/EXTRA NOTES

Notes

He hath eaten me out of house and home.

—William Shakespeare

17

FAMILY ROOM

FLOOR COVERING

MEASUREMENTS • Floor

Width _____ X Depth _____ = _____ sq. ft.

TYPE & MATERIAL • Floor Covering

Description *(nylon carpet, ceramic tile, etc.)* _____
Brand & pattern _____
Color & number _____
Backing type _____ Pad type _____

PURCHASE • Floor Covering

Retailer _____
Date _____ Cost/unit $ _____
No. of units _____ Total cost $ _____
Warranty _____

INSTALLATION • Floor Covering

Installer _____
Date _____ Cost $ _____

CLEANING & REFINISHING • Floor Covering

Company _____
Date _____ Cost $ _____
Company _____
Date _____ Cost $ _____

CEILING COVERING

TYPE & MATERIAL • Ceiling Covering

Description *(paint, spray texture, etc.)* _____
Brand & pattern _____
Color & number _____

PURCHASE • Ceiling Covering

Retailer _____
Date _____ Cost/unit $ _____
No. of units _____ Total cost $ _____
Warranty _____

INSTALLATION • Ceiling Covering

Installer _____
Date _____ Cost $ _____

WALL COVERING

MEASUREMENTS • Walls

North: Width _____ X Height _____ = _____ sq. ft.
South: Width _____ X Height _____ = _____ sq. ft.
East: Width _____ X Height _____ = _____ sq. ft.
West: Width _____ X Height _____ = _____ sq. ft.

▶ TYPE & MATERIAL • First Wall Covering

Description *(paint, paper, paneling, etc.)* _____
Brand & pattern _____
Color & number _____

PURCHASE • First Wall Covering

Retailer _____
Date _____ Cost/unit $ _____
No. of units _____ Total cost $ _____
Warranty _____

INSTALLATION • First Wall Covering

Installer _____
Date _____ Cost $ _____

CLEANING & REFINISHING • First Wall Covering

Company _____
Date _____ Cost $ _____
Company _____
Date _____ Cost $ _____

▶ TYPE & MATERIAL • Second Wall Covering

Description *(paint, paper, paneling, etc.)* _____
Brand & pattern _____
Color & number _____

PURCHASE • Second Wall Covering

Retailer _____
Date _____ Cost/unit $ _____
No. of units _____ Total cost $ _____
Warranty _____

INSTALLATION • Second Wall Covering

Installer _____
Date _____ Cost $ _____

CLEANING & REFINISHING • Second Wall Covering

Company _____
Date _____ Cost $ _____
Company _____
Date _____ Cost $ _____

FAMILY ROOM

Notes

_____
_____
_____
_____
_____
_____
_____
_____
_____
_____
_____
_____
_____
_____
_____
_____
_____
_____
_____

▶ **Tip:** You can clean up spilled liquid on your carpet by immediately blotting up as much up as possible with a soft, white, absorbent cloth or napkin. Do not rub! Remember, the longer a stain sits, the harder it will be to get out.

FAMILY ROOM

✎ Notes

_____
_____
_____
_____
_____
_____
_____
_____
_____
_____
_____
_____
_____
_____
_____
_____
_____
_____
_____
_____
_____
_____
_____
_____
_____
_____
_____
_____
_____
_____
_____

WINDOWS

MEASUREMENTS • Windows

Window 1: Width _____ Height _____
Window 2: Width _____ Height _____
Window 3: Width _____ Height _____

TYPE & MATERIAL • Windows

Description *(vinyl casement, etc.)* _____
Brand & model _____

PURCHASE • Windows

Retailer _____
Date _____ Cost/unit $ _____
No. of units _____ Total cost $ _____
Warranty _____

INSTALLATION • Windows

Installer _____
Date _____ Cost $ _____

WINDOW TREATMENTS

MEASUREMENTS • Window Treatments

Treatment 1: Width _____ X Height _____ = _____ sq. ft.
Treatment 2: Width _____ X Height _____ = _____ sq. ft.
Treatment 3: Width _____ X Height _____ = _____ sq. ft.

TYPE & MATERIAL • Window Treatments

Description *(draperies, blinds, etc.)* _____
Brand & model _____
Color & number _____
Description *(draperies, blinds, etc.)* _____
Brand & model _____
Color & number _____

PURCHASE • Window Treatments

Retailer _____
Date _____ Cost/unit $ _____
No. of units _____ Total cost $ _____
Warranty _____

INSTALLATION • Window Treatments

Installer _____
Date _____ Cost $ _____

CLEANING & REFINISHING • Window Treatments

Company _____
Date _____ Cost $ _____

DOORS

MEASUREMENTS • Doors

First Door: Second Door:
Width _____ Height _____   Width _____ Height _____

▶ **TYPE & MATERIAL** • First Door
Description *(oak, masonite, etc.)* _____
Brand & style _____
Color & number _____
Hardware description _____

PURCHASE • First Door
Retailer _____
Date _____ Cost/unit $ _____
No. of units _____ Total cost $ _____
Warranty _____

INSTALLATION • First Door
Installer _____
Date _____ Cost $ _____

CLEANING & REFINISHING • First Door
Company _____
  Date _____ Cost $ _____
Company _____
  Date _____ Cost $ _____

▶ **TYPE & MATERIAL** • Second Door
Description *(oak, masonite, etc.)* _____
Brand & style _____
Color & number _____
Hardware description _____

PURCHASE • Second Door
Retailer _____
Date _____ Cost/unit $ _____
No. of units _____ Total cost $ _____
Warranty _____

INSTALLATION • Second Door
Installer _____
Date _____ Cost $ _____

CLEANING & REFINISHING • Second Door
Company _____
  Date _____ Cost $ _____
Company _____
  Date _____ Cost $ _____

FAMILY ROOM

Notes
_____
_____
_____
_____
_____
_____
_____
_____
_____
_____
_____
_____
_____
_____
_____
_____
_____
_____
_____
_____
_____

Home is the place where, when you have to go there, they have to take you in.

—Robert Frost

21

FAMILY ROOM

✎ *Notes*

SAMPLES

Attach Swatch or Daub Paint Here

CLOSETS

DIAGRAMS/EXTRA NOTES

BEDROOM 1

FLOOR COVERING

MEASUREMENTS • Floor
Width _____ X Depth _____ = _____ sq. ft.

TYPE & MATERIAL • Floor Covering
Description *(nylon carpet, ceramic tile, etc.)* _____
Brand & pattern _____
Color & number _____
Backing type _____ Pad type _____

PURCHASE • Floor Covering
Retailer _____
Date _____ Cost/unit $ _____
No. of units _____ Total cost $ _____
Warranty _____

INSTALLATION • Floor Covering
Installer _____
Date _____ Cost $ _____

CLEANING & REFINISHING • Floor Covering
Company _____
Date _____ Cost $ _____
Company _____
Date _____ Cost $ _____

CEILING COVERING

TYPE & MATERIAL • Ceiling Covering
Description *(paint, spray texture, etc.)* _____
Brand & pattern _____
Color & number _____

PURCHASE • Ceiling Covering
Retailer _____
Date _____ Cost/unit $ _____
No. of units _____ Total cost $ _____
Warranty _____

INSTALLATION • Ceiling Covering
Installer _____
Date _____ Cost $ _____

Notes
_____
_____
_____
_____
_____
_____
_____
_____
_____
_____
_____
_____
_____
_____
_____
_____
_____

 Tip: Squeaky floorboards? Sprinkle a generous amount of talcum powder wherever the floor makes noise. Work the powder into the joints and around any exposed nail heads. It's a great temporary solution that usually lasts for several weeks.

BEDROOM 1

_____

Notes

_____
_____
_____
_____
_____
_____
_____
_____
_____
_____
_____
_____
_____
_____
_____
_____
_____
_____
_____
_____
_____
_____
_____
_____
_____
_____
_____
_____

24

WALL COVERING

MEASUREMENTS • Walls

North: Width _____ X Height _____ = _____ sq. ft.
South: Width _____ X Height _____ = _____ sq. ft.
East: Width _____ X Height _____ = _____ sq. ft.
West: Width _____ X Height _____ = _____ sq. ft.

▶ **TYPE & MATERIAL** • First Wall Covering
Description _(paint, paper, paneling, etc.)_ _____
Brand & pattern _____
Color & number _____

PURCHASE • First Wall Covering
Retailer _____
Date _____ Cost/unit $ _____
No. of units _____ Total cost $ _____
Warranty _____

INSTALLATION • First Wall Covering
Installer _____
Date _____ Cost $ _____

CLEANING & REFINISHING • First Wall Covering
Company _____
   Date _____ Cost $ _____
Company _____
   Date _____ Cost $ _____

▶ **TYPE & MATERIAL** • Second Wall Covering
Description _(paint, paper, paneling, etc.)_ _____
Brand & pattern _____
Color & number _____

PURCHASE • Second Wall Covering
Retailer _____
Date _____ Cost/unit $ _____
No. of units _____ Total cost $ _____
Warranty _____

INSTALLATION • Second Wall Covering
Installer _____
Date _____ Cost $ _____

CLEANING & REFINISHING • Second Wall Covering
Company _____
   Date _____ Cost $ _____
Company _____
   Date _____ Cost $ _____

WINDOWS

MEASUREMENTS • Windows

Window 1: Width _____ Height _____
Window 2: Width _____ Height _____
Window 3: Width _____ Height _____

TYPE & MATERIAL • Windows

Description *(vinyl casement, etc.)* _____
Brand & model _____

PURCHASE • Windows

Retailer _____
Date _____ Cost/unit $ _____
No. of units _____ Total cost $ _____
Warranty _____

INSTALLATION • Windows

Installer _____
Date _____ Cost $ _____

WINDOW TREATMENTS

MEASUREMENTS • Window Treatments

Treatment 1: Width ____ X Height ____ = ____ sq. ft.
Treatment 2: Width ____ X Height ____ = ____ sq. ft.
Treatment 3: Width ____ X Height ____ = ____ sq. ft.

TYPE & MATERIAL • Window Treatments

Description *(draperies, blinds, etc.)* _____
  Brand & model _____
  Color & number _____
Description *(draperies, blinds, etc.)* _____
  Brand & model _____
  Color & number _____

PURCHASE • Window Treatments

Retailer _____
Date _____ Cost/unit $ _____
No. of units _____ Total cost $ _____
Warranty _____

INSTALLATION • Window Treatments

Installer _____
Date _____ Cost $ _____

CLEANING & REFINISHING • Window Treatments

Company _____
  Date _____ Cost $ _____

Notes

_____
_____
_____
_____
_____
_____
_____
_____
_____
_____
_____
_____
_____
_____
_____
_____
_____
_____
_____

▶ **Tip:** Why not use your best asset when decorating or remodeling . . . you! Be creative!

25

BEDROOM 1

Notes

DOORS

MEASUREMENTS • Doors

First Door: Second Door:
Width _____ Height _____   Width _____ Height _____

▶ TYPE & MATERIAL • First Door

Description *(oak, masonite, etc.)* _____
Brand & style _____
Color & number _____
Hardware description _____

PURCHASE • First Door

Retailer _____
Date _____   Cost/unit $ _____
No. of units _____   Total cost $ _____
Warranty _____

INSTALLATION • First Door

Installer _____
Date _____   Cost $ _____

CLEANING & REFINISHING • First Door

Company _____
  Date _____   Cost $ _____
Company _____
  Date _____   Cost $ _____

▶ TYPE & MATERIAL • Second Door

Description *(oak, masonite, etc.)* _____
Brand & style _____
Color & number _____
Hardware description _____

PURCHASE • Second Door

Retailer _____
Date _____   Cost/unit $ _____
No. of units _____   Total cost $ _____
Warranty _____

INSTALLATION • Second Door

Installer _____
Date _____   Cost $ _____

CLEANING & REFINISHING • Second Door

Company _____
  Date _____   Cost $ _____
Company _____
  Date _____   Cost $ _____

SAMPLES

Attach Swatch or Daub Paint Here

CLOSETS

DIAGRAMS/EXTRA NOTES

Notes

ET, phone home.

—Melissa Mathison,
U.S. screenwriter

BEDROOM 2

FLOOR COVERING

MEASUREMENTS • Floor

Width _____ X Depth _____ = _____ sq. ft.

TYPE & MATERIAL • Floor Covering

Description *(nylon carpet, ceramic tile, etc.)* _____
Brand & pattern _____
Color & number _____
Backing type _____ Pad type _____

PURCHASE • Floor Covering

Retailer _____
Date _____ Cost/unit $ _____
No. of units _____ Total cost $ _____
Warranty _____

INSTALLATION • Floor Covering

Installer _____
Date _____ Cost $ _____

CLEANING & REFINISHING • Floor Covering

Company _____
  Date _____ Cost $ _____
Company _____
  Date _____ Cost $ _____

CEILING COVERING

TYPE & MATERIAL • Ceiling Covering

Description *(paint, spray texture, etc.)* _____
Brand & pattern _____
Color & number _____

PURCHASE • Ceiling Covering

Retailer _____
Date _____ Cost/unit $ _____
No. of units _____ Total cost $ _____
Warranty _____

INSTALLATION • Ceiling Covering

Installer _____
Date _____ Cost $ _____

Notes

WALL COVERING

MEASUREMENTS • Walls

North: Width _____ X Height _____ = _____ sq. ft.
South: Width _____ X Height _____ = _____ sq. ft.
East: Width _____ X Height _____ = _____ sq. ft.
West: Width _____ X Height _____ = _____ sq. ft.

▶ **TYPE & MATERIAL** • First Wall Covering
Description *(paint, paper, paneling, etc.)* _____
Brand & pattern _____
Color & number _____

PURCHASE • First Wall Covering
Retailer _____
Date _____ Cost/unit $ _____
No. of units _____ Total cost $ _____
Warranty _____

INSTALLATION • First Wall Covering
Installer _____
Date _____ Cost $ _____

CLEANING & REFINISHING • First Wall Covering
Company _____
Date _____ Cost $ _____
Company _____
Date _____ Cost $ _____

▶ **TYPE & MATERIAL** • Second Wall Covering
Description *(paint, paper, paneling, etc.)* _____
Brand & pattern _____
Color & number _____

PURCHASE • Second Wall Covering
Retailer _____
Date _____ Cost/unit $ _____
No. of units _____ Total cost $ _____
Warranty _____

INSTALLATION • Second Wall Covering
Installer _____
Date _____ Cost $ _____

CLEANING & REFINISHING • Second Wall Covering
Company _____
Date _____ Cost $ _____
Company _____
Date _____ Cost $ _____

Notes

▶ **Tip:** Baking soda can be used as a mild abrasive on surfaces such as fiberglass and glass, where using standard abrasive cleaners causes scratching.

29

BEDROOM 2

WINDOWS

MEASUREMENTS • Windows

Window 1: Width _____ Height _____
Window 2: Width _____ Height _____
Window 3: Width _____ Height _____

TYPE & MATERIAL • Windows

Description *(vinyl casement, etc.)* _____
Brand & model _____

PURCHASE • Windows

Retailer _____
Date _____ Cost/unit $ _____
No. of units _____ Total cost $ _____
Warranty _____

INSTALLATION • Windows

Installer _____
Date _____ Cost $ _____

WINDOW TREATMENTS

MEASUREMENTS • Window Treatments

Treatment 1: Width _____ X Height _____ = _____ sq. ft.
Treatment 2: Width _____ X Height _____ = _____ sq. ft.
Treatment 3: Width _____ X Height _____ = _____ sq. ft.

TYPE & MATERIAL • Window Treatments

Description *(draperies, blinds, etc.)* _____
  Brand & model _____
  Color & number _____
Description *(draperies, blinds, etc.)* _____
  Brand & model _____
  Color & number _____

PURCHASE • Window Treatments

Retailer _____
Date _____ Cost/unit $ _____
No. of units _____ Total cost $ _____
Warranty _____

INSTALLATION • Window Treatments

Installer _____
Date _____ Cost $ _____

CLEANING & REFINISHING • Window Treatments

Company _____
  Date _____ Cost $ _____

DOORS

MEASUREMENTS • Doors

First Door: Second Door:

Width _____ Height _____   Width _____ Height _____

▶ **TYPE & MATERIAL** • First Door

Description *(oak, masonite, etc.)* _____

Brand & style _____

Color & number _____

Hardware description _____

PURCHASE • First Door

Retailer _____

Date _____ Cost/unit $ _____

No. of units _____ Total cost $ _____

Warranty _____

INSTALLATION • First Door

Installer _____

Date _____ Cost $ _____

CLEANING & REFINISHING • First Door

Company _____

Date _____ Cost $ _____

Company _____

Date _____ Cost $ _____

▶ **TYPE & MATERIAL** • Second Door

Description *(oak, masonite, etc.)* _____

Brand & style _____

Color & number _____

Hardware description _____

PURCHASE • Second Door

Retailer _____

Date _____ Cost/unit $ _____

No. of units _____ Total cost $ _____

Warranty _____

INSTALLATION • Second Door

Installer _____

Date _____ Cost $ _____

CLEANING & REFINISHING • Second Door

Company _____

Date _____ Cost $ _____

Company _____

Date _____ Cost $ _____

Notes

_____
_____
_____
_____
_____
_____
_____
_____
_____
_____
_____
_____
_____
_____
_____
_____

Home again, I can groan, scratch, and talk to myself.

—Mason Cooley

31

BEDROOM 2

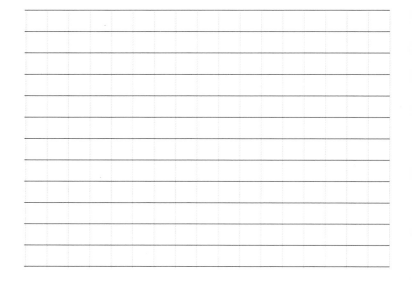

✎ Notes

SAMPLES

Attach Swatch or Daub Paint Here

CLOSETS

DIAGRAMS/EXTRA NOTES

BEDROOM 3

FLOOR COVERING

MEASUREMENTS • Floor
Width _____ X Depth _____ = _____ sq. ft.

TYPE & MATERIAL • Floor Covering
Description *(nylon carpet, ceramic tile, etc.)* _____
Brand & pattern _____
Color & number _____
Backing type _____ Pad type _____

PURCHASE • Floor Covering
Retailer _____
Date _____ Cost/unit $ _____
No. of units _____ Total cost $ _____
Warranty _____

INSTALLATION • Floor Covering
Installer _____
Date _____ Cost $ _____

CLEANING & REFINISHING • Floor Covering
Company _____
Date _____ Cost $ _____
Company _____
Date _____ Cost $ _____

CEILING COVERING

TYPE & MATERIAL • Ceiling Covering
Description *(paint, spray texture, etc.)* _____
Brand & pattern _____
Color & number _____

PURCHASE • Ceiling Covering
Retailer _____
Date _____ Cost/unit $ _____
No. of units _____ Total cost $ _____
Warranty _____

INSTALLATION • Ceiling Covering
Installer _____
Date _____ Cost $ _____

Notes
_____
_____
_____
_____
_____
_____
_____
_____
_____
_____
_____
_____
_____
_____
_____
_____

▶ **Tip:** Keep key locks lubricated by "coloring" the key with a pencil and inserting it into the lock a few times. The graphite from the pencil will lubricate the lock.

BEDROOM 3

Notes

_____
_____
_____
_____
_____
_____
_____
_____
_____
_____
_____
_____
_____
_____
_____
_____
_____
_____
_____
_____
_____
_____
_____
_____
_____
_____
_____
_____
_____

WALL COVERING

MEASUREMENTS • Walls

North:	Width _____	X Height _____	= _____ sq. ft.
South:	Width _____	X Height _____	= _____ sq. ft.
East:	Width _____	X Height _____	= _____ sq. ft.
West:	Width _____	X Height _____	= _____ sq. ft.

▶ **TYPE & MATERIAL** • First Wall Covering
Description *(paint, paper, paneling, etc.)* _____
Brand & pattern _____
Color & number _____

PURCHASE • First Wall Covering
Retailer _____
Date _____ Cost/unit $ _____
No. of units _____ Total cost $ _____
Warranty _____

INSTALLATION • First Wall Covering
Installer _____
Date _____ Cost $ _____

CLEANING & REFINISHING • First Wall Covering
Company _____
Date _____ Cost $ _____
Company _____
Date _____ Cost $ _____

▶ **TYPE & MATERIAL** • Second Wall Covering
Description *(paint, paper, paneling, etc.)* _____
Brand & pattern _____
Color & number _____

PURCHASE • Second Wall Covering
Retailer _____
Date _____ Cost/unit $ _____
No. of units _____ Total cost $ _____
Warranty _____

INSTALLATION • Second Wall Covering
Installer _____
Date _____ Cost $ _____

CLEANING & REFINISHING • Second Wall Covering
Company _____
Date _____ Cost $ _____
Company _____
Date _____ Cost $ _____

WINDOWS

MEASUREMENTS • Windows

Window 1: Width _____ Height _____
Window 2: Width _____ Height _____
Window 3: Width _____ Height _____

TYPE & MATERIAL • Windows

Description *(vinyl casement, etc.)* _____
Brand & model _____

PURCHASE • Windows

Retailer _____
Date _____ Cost/unit $ _____
No. of units _____ Total cost $ _____
Warranty _____

INSTALLATION • Windows

Installer _____
Date _____ Cost $ _____

WINDOW TREATMENTS

MEASUREMENTS • Window Treatments

Treatment 1: Width _____ X Height _____ = _____ sq. ft.
Treatment 2: Width _____ X Height _____ = _____ sq. ft.
Treatment 3: Width _____ X Height _____ = _____ sq. ft.

TYPE & MATERIAL • Window Treatments

Description *(draperies, blinds, etc.)* _____
    Brand & model _____
    Color & number _____
Description *(draperies, blinds, etc.)* _____
    Brand & model _____
    Color & number _____

PURCHASE • Window Treatments

Retailer _____
Date _____ Cost/unit $ _____
No. of units _____ Total cost $ _____
Warranty _____

INSTALLATION • Window Treatments

Installer _____
Date _____ Cost $ _____

CLEANING & REFINISHING • Window Treatments

Company _____
    Date _____ Cost $ _____

Notes

Tip: After you clean your windows, rub them down with a cloth that's been dampened with rubbing alcohol. No streaks!

35

BEDROOM 3

DOORS

MEASUREMENTS • Doors

First Door: Second Door:
Width _____ Height _____   Width _____ Height _____

▶ **TYPE & MATERIAL** • First Door
Description *(oak, masonite, etc.)* _____
Brand & style _____
Color & number _____
Hardware description _____

PURCHASE • First Door
Retailer _____
Date _____ Cost/unit $ _____
No. of units _____ Total cost $ _____
Warranty _____

INSTALLATION • First Door
Installer _____
Date _____ Cost $ _____

CLEANING & REFINISHING • First Door
Company _____
Date _____ Cost $ _____
Company _____
Date _____ Cost $ _____

▶ **TYPE & MATERIAL** • Second Door
Description *(oak, masonite, etc.)* _____
Brand & style _____
Color & number _____
Hardware description _____

PURCHASE • Second Door
Retailer _____
Date _____ Cost/unit $ _____
No. of units _____ Total cost $ _____
Warranty _____

INSTALLATION • Second Door
Installer _____
Date _____ Cost $ _____

CLEANING & REFINISHING • Second Door
Company _____
Date _____ Cost $ _____
Company _____
Date _____ Cost $ _____

SAMPLES

Attach Swatch or Daub Paint Here

CLOSETS

DIAGRAMS/EXTRA NOTES

Notes

Tip: Make the best use of your storage space. You'll find there are many closet organizing systems available on the market, or you could build your own and customize it to your needs.

BEDROOM 4

FLOOR COVERING

MEASUREMENTS • Floor
Width _____ X Depth _____ = _____ sq. ft.

TYPE & MATERIAL • Floor Covering
Description *(nylon carpet, ceramic tile, etc.)* _____
Brand & pattern _____
Color & number _____
Backing type _____ Pad type _____

PURCHASE • Floor Covering
Retailer _____
Date _____ Cost/unit $ _____
No. of units _____ Total cost $ _____
Warranty _____

INSTALLATION • Floor Covering
Installer _____
Date _____ Cost $ _____

CLEANING & REFINISHING • Floor Covering
Company _____
Date _____ Cost $ _____
Company _____
Date _____ Cost $ _____

CEILING COVERING

TYPE & MATERIAL • Ceiling Covering
Description *(paint, spray texture, etc.)* _____
Brand & pattern _____
Color & number _____

PURCHASE • Ceiling Covering
Retailer _____
Date _____ Cost/unit $ _____
No. of units _____ Total cost $ _____
Warranty _____

INSTALLATION • Ceiling Covering
Installer _____
Date _____ Cost $ _____

WALL COVERING

MEASUREMENTS • Walls

North:	Width	X Height	=	sq. ft.
South:	Width	X Height	=	sq. ft.
East:	Width	X Height	=	sq. ft.
West:	Width	X Height	=	sq. ft.

▶ **TYPE & MATERIAL** • First Wall Covering

Description *(paint, paper, paneling, etc.)*
Brand & pattern
Color & number

PURCHASE • First Wall Covering

Retailer
Date   Cost/unit $
No. of units   Total cost $
Warranty

INSTALLATION • First Wall Covering

Installer
Date   Cost $

CLEANING & REFINISHING • First Wall Covering

Company
    Date   Cost $
Company
    Date   Cost $

▶ **TYPE & MATERIAL** • Second Wall Covering

Description *(paint, paper, paneling, etc.)*
Brand & pattern
Color & number

PURCHASE • Second Wall Covering

Retailer
Date   Cost/unit $
No. of units   Total cost $
Warranty

INSTALLATION • Second Wall Covering

Installer
Date   Cost $

CLEANING & REFINISHING • Second Wall Covering

Company
    Date   Cost $
Company
    Date   Cost $

Notes

HOW TO

MATCH A PAINT COLOR

The majority of paint retailers have the ability to scan a paint chip and electronically match the color. Chip off a dime sized or larger sample from a discrete area of the room. Take the sample to your paint retailer and they will do the rest!

39

BEDROOM 4

Notes

WINDOWS

MEASUREMENTS • Windows
    Window 1: Width _____ Height _____
    Window 2: Width _____ Height _____
    Window 3: Width _____ Height _____

TYPE & MATERIAL • Windows
    Description *(vinyl casement, etc.)* _____
    Brand & model _____

PURCHASE • Windows
    Retailer _____
    Date _____ Cost/unit $ _____
    No. of units _____ Total cost $ _____
    Warranty _____

INSTALLATION • Windows
    Installer _____
    Date _____ Cost $ _____

WINDOW TREATMENTS

MEASUREMENTS • Window Treatments
    Treatment 1: Width _____ X Height _____ = _____ sq. ft.
    Treatment 2: Width _____ X Height _____ = _____ sq. ft.
    Treatment 3: Width _____ X Height _____ = _____ sq. ft.

TYPE & MATERIAL • Window Treatments
    Description *(draperies, blinds, etc.)* _____
      Brand & model _____
      Color & number _____
    Description *(draperies, blinds, etc.)* _____
      Brand & model _____
      Color & number _____

PURCHASE • Window Treatments
    Retailer _____
    Date _____ Cost/unit $ _____
    No. of units _____ Total cost $ _____
    Warranty _____

INSTALLATION • Window Treatments
    Installer _____
    Date _____ Cost $ _____

CLEANING & REFINISHING • Window Treatments
    Company _____
      Date _____ Cost $ _____

40

DOORS

MEASUREMENTS • Doors

First Door: Second Door:
Width _____ Height _____   Width _____ Height _____

▶ **TYPE & MATERIAL** • First Door
Description *(oak, masonite, etc.)* _____
Brand & style _____
Color & number _____
Hardware description _____

PURCHASE • First Door
Retailer _____
Date _____ Cost/unit $ _____
No. of units _____ Total cost $ _____
Warranty _____

INSTALLATION • First Door
Installer _____
Date _____ Cost $ _____

CLEANING & REFINISHING • First Door
Company _____
   Date _____ Cost $ _____
Company _____
   Date _____ Cost $ _____

▶ **TYPE & MATERIAL** • Second Door
Description *(oak, masonite, etc.)* _____
Brand & style _____
Color & number _____
Hardware description _____

PURCHASE • Second Door
Retailer _____
Date _____ Cost/unit $ _____
No. of units _____ Total cost $ _____
Warranty _____

INSTALLATION • Second Door
Installer _____
Date _____ Cost $ _____

CLEANING & REFINISHING • Second Door
Company _____
   Date _____ Cost $ _____
Company _____
   Date _____ Cost $ _____

Notes

▶ **Tip:** You can use olive oil to clean paint from your skin. It works great, and softens your hands at the same time!

41

BEDROOM 4

Notes

Attach Swatch or Daub Paint Here

CLOSETS

DIAGRAMS/EXTRA NOTES

42

BATHROOM 1

FLOOR COVERING

MEASUREMENTS • Floor

Width _____ X Depth _____ = _____ sq. ft.

TYPE & MATERIAL • Floor Covering

Description *(nylon carpet, ceramic tile, etc.)* _____
Brand & pattern _____
Color & number _____
Backing type _____ Pad type _____

PURCHASE • Floor Covering

Retailer _____
Date _____ Cost/unit $ _____
No. of units _____ Total cost $ _____
Warranty _____

INSTALLATION • Floor Covering

Installer _____
Date _____ Cost $ _____

CLEANING & REFINISHING • Floor Covering

Company _____
    Date _____ Cost $ _____
Company _____
    Date _____ Cost $ _____

CEILING COVERING

TYPE & MATERIAL • Ceiling Covering

Description *(paint, spray texture, etc.)* _____
Brand & pattern _____
Color & number _____

PURCHASE • Ceiling Covering

Retailer _____
Date _____ Cost/unit $ _____
No. of units _____ Total cost $ _____
Warranty _____

INSTALLATION • Ceiling Covering

Installer _____
Date _____ Cost $ _____

Notes
_____
_____
_____
_____
_____
_____
_____
_____
_____
_____
_____
_____
_____
_____

Tip: When remodeling your bathroom, you'll save money by leaving the sink, bathtub, and toilet where they are. Moving fixtures is costly.

BATHROOM 1

Notes

_____

_____

_____

_____

_____

_____

_____

_____

_____

_____

_____

_____

_____

_____

_____

_____

_____

_____

_____

_____

_____

_____

_____

_____

_____

WALL COVERING

MEASUREMENTS • Walls

North:	Width _____	X Height _____	= _____	sq. ft.
South:	Width _____	X Height _____	= _____	sq. ft.
East:	Width _____	X Height _____	= _____	sq. ft.
West:	Width _____	X Height _____	= _____	sq. ft.

▶ **TYPE & MATERIAL** • First Wall Covering

Description *(paint, paper, paneling, etc.)* _____

Brand & pattern _____

Color & number _____

PURCHASE • First Wall Covering

Retailer _____

Date _____   Cost/unit $ _____

No. of units _____   Total cost $ _____

Warranty _____

INSTALLATION • First Wall Covering

Installer _____

Date _____   Cost $ _____

CLEANING & REFINISHING • First Wall Covering

Company _____

Date _____   Cost $ _____

Company _____

Date _____   Cost $ _____

▶ **TYPE & MATERIAL** • Second Wall Covering

Description *(paint, paper, paneling, etc.)* _____

Brand & pattern _____

Color & number _____

PURCHASE • Second Wall Covering

Retailer _____

Date _____   Cost/unit $ _____

No. of units _____   Total cost $ _____

Warranty _____

INSTALLATION • Second Wall Covering

Installer _____

Date _____   Cost $ _____

CLEANING & REFINISHING • Second Wall Covering

Company _____

Date _____   Cost $ _____

Company _____

Date _____   Cost $ _____

WINDOWS

MEASUREMENTS • Windows

Window 1: Width _____ Height _____
Window 2: Width _____ Height _____

TYPE & MATERIAL • Windows

Description *(vinyl casement, etc.)* _____
Brand & model _____

PURCHASE • Windows

Retailer _____
Date _____ Cost/unit $ _____
No. of units _____ Total cost $ _____
Warranty _____

INSTALLATION • Windows

Installer _____
Date _____ Cost $ _____

WINDOW TREATMENTS

MEASUREMENTS • Window Treatments

Treatment 1: Width ___ X Height ___ = ___ sq. ft.
Treatment 2: Width ___ X Height ___ = ___ sq. ft.

TYPE & MATERIAL • Window Treatments

Description *(draperies, blinds, etc.)* _____
Brand & model _____
Color & number _____
Description *(draperies, blinds, etc.)* _____
Brand & model _____
Color & number _____

PURCHASE • Window Treatments

Retailer _____
Date _____ Cost/unit $ _____
No. of units _____ Total cost $ _____
Warranty _____

INSTALLATION • Window Treatments

Installer _____
Date _____ Cost $ _____

CLEANING & REFINISHING • Window Treatments

Company _____
Date _____ Cost $ _____
Company _____
Date _____ Cost $ _____

Notes

Tip: You can use cotton balls for lots of things.
—Andrew, age 8

45

BATHROOM 1

✏️ Notes

_____

_____

_____

_____

_____

_____

_____

_____

_____

_____

_____

_____

_____

_____

_____

_____

_____

_____

_____

_____

_____

_____

_____

_____

_____

DOOR

MEASUREMENTS • Door
Width _____ Height _____

TYPE & MATERIAL • Door
Description *(oak, masonite, etc.)* _____
Brand & style _____
Color & number _____
Hardware description _____

PURCHASE • Door
Retailer _____
Date _____ Cost/unit $ _____
No. of units _____ Total cost $ _____
Warranty _____

INSTALLATION • Door
Installer _____
Date _____ Cost $ _____

CLEANING & REFINISHING • Door
Company _____
Date _____ Cost $ _____

SAMPLES

Attach Swatch or Daub Paint Here

FIXTURES

CLOSETS

DIAGRAMS/EXTRA NOTES

Notes

> *A home without a cat—and a well fed, well petted, and properly revered cat,—may be a home, perhaps, but how can it prove title?*
>
> —Mark Twain,
> [Samuel Clemens]

BATHROOM 2

Notes

_____
_____
_____
_____
_____
_____
_____
_____
_____
_____
_____
_____
_____
_____
_____
_____
_____
_____
_____
_____
_____
_____
_____
_____
_____
_____

FLOOR COVERING

MEASUREMENTS • Floor
Width _____ X Depth _____ = _____ sq. ft.

TYPE & MATERIAL • Floor Covering
Description *(nylon carpet, ceramic tile, etc.)* _____
Brand & pattern _____
Color & number _____
Backing type _____ Pad type _____

PURCHASE • Floor Covering
Retailer _____
Date _____ Cost/unit $ _____
No. of units _____ Total cost $ _____
Warranty _____

INSTALLATION • Floor Covering
Installer _____
Date _____ Cost $ _____

CLEANING & REFINISHING • Floor Covering
Company _____
Date _____ Cost $ _____
Company _____
Date _____ Cost $ _____

CEILING COVERING

TYPE & MATERIAL • Ceiling Covering
Description *(paint, spray texture, etc.)* _____
Brand & pattern _____
Color & number _____

PURCHASE • Ceiling Covering
Retailer _____
Date _____ Cost/unit $ _____
No. of units _____ Total cost $ _____
Warranty _____

INSTALLATION • Ceiling Covering
Installer _____
Date _____ Cost $ _____

WALL COVERING

MEASUREMENTS • Walls

North: Width _____ X Height _____ = _____ sq. ft.
South: Width _____ X Height _____ = _____ sq. ft.
East: Width _____ X Height _____ = _____ sq. ft.
West: Width _____ X Height _____ = _____ sq. ft.

▶ **TYPE & MATERIAL** • First Wall Covering
Description *(paint, paper, paneling, etc.)* _____
Brand & pattern _____
Color & number _____

PURCHASE • First Wall Covering
Retailer _____
Date _____ Cost/unit $ _____
No. of units _____ Total cost $ _____
Warranty _____

INSTALLATION • First Wall Covering
Installer _____
Date _____ Cost $ _____

CLEANING & REFINISHING • First Wall Covering
Company _____
Date _____ Cost $ _____
Company _____
Date _____ Cost $ _____

▶ **TYPE & MATERIAL** • Second Wall Covering
Description *(paint, paper, paneling, etc.)* _____
Brand & pattern _____
Color & number _____

PURCHASE • Second Wall Covering
Retailer _____
Date _____ Cost/unit $ _____
No. of units _____ Total cost $ _____
Warranty _____

INSTALLATION • Second Wall Covering
Installer _____
Date _____ Cost $ _____

CLEANING & REFINISHING • Second Wall Covering
Company _____
Date _____ Cost $ _____
Company _____
Date _____ Cost $ _____

Notes
_____
_____
_____
_____
_____
_____
_____
_____
_____
_____
_____
_____
_____
_____
_____
_____
_____
_____
_____

Tip: Take care of your carpet! It's best if you vacuum frequently to prevent soil buildup. Carpet manufacturers recommend 3-7 strokes in the forward and backward direction with a high quality vacuum cleaner.

BATHROOM 2

WINDOWS

MEASUREMENTS • Windows
Window 1: Width _____ Height _____
Window 2: Width _____ Height _____

TYPE & MATERIAL • Windows
Description *(vinyl casement, etc.)* _____
Brand & model _____

PURCHASE • Windows
Retailer _____
Date _____ Cost/unit $ _____
No. of units _____ Total cost $ _____
Warranty _____

INSTALLATION • Windows
Installer _____
Date _____ Cost $ _____

WINDOW TREATMENTS

MEASUREMENTS • Window Treatments
Treatment 1: Width _____ X Height _____ = _____ sq. ft.
Treatment 2: Width _____ X Height _____ = _____ sq. ft.

TYPE & MATERIAL • Window Treatments
Description *(draperies, blinds, etc.)* _____
Brand & model _____
Color & number _____
Description *(draperies, blinds, etc.)* _____
Brand & model _____
Color & number _____

PURCHASE • Window Treatments
Retailer _____
Date _____ Cost/unit $ _____
No. of units _____ Total cost $ _____
Warranty _____

INSTALLATION • Window Treatments
Installer _____
Date _____ Cost $ _____

CLEANING & REFINISHING • Window Treatments
Company _____
Date _____ Cost $ _____
Company _____
Date _____ Cost $ _____

DOOR

MEASUREMENTS • Door

Width _____ Height _____

TYPE & MATERIAL • Door

Description *(oak, masonite, etc.)* _____

Brand & style _____

Color & number _____

Hardware description _____

PURCHASE • Door

Retailer _____

Date _____ Cost/unit $ _____

No. of units _____ Total cost $ _____

Warranty _____

INSTALLATION • Door

Installer _____

Date _____ Cost $ _____

CLEANING & REFINISHING • Door

Company _____

Date _____ Cost $ _____

SAMPLES

Attach Swatch or Daub Paint Here

Notes

Any old place I can hang my hat is home sweet home to me.

—William Jerome

BATHROOM 2

Notes

CLOSETS

DIAGRAMS/EXTRA NOTES

52

BATHROOM 3

FLOOR COVERING

MEASUREMENTS • Floor

Width _____ X Depth _____ = _____ sq. ft.

TYPE & MATERIAL • Floor Covering

Description *(nylon carpet, ceramic tile, etc.)* _____
Brand & pattern _____
Color & number _____
Backing type _____ Pad type _____

PURCHASE • Floor Covering

Retailer _____
Date _____ Cost/unit $ _____
No. of units _____ Total cost $ _____
Warranty _____

INSTALLATION • Floor Covering

Installer _____
Date _____ Cost $ _____

CLEANING & REFINISHING • Floor Covering

Company _____
  Date _____ Cost $ _____
Company _____
  Date _____ Cost $ _____

CEILING COVERING

TYPE & MATERIAL • Ceiling Covering

Description *(paint, spray texture, etc.)* _____
Brand & pattern _____
Color & number _____

PURCHASE • Ceiling Covering

Retailer _____
Date _____ Cost/unit $ _____
No. of units _____ Total cost $ _____
Warranty _____

INSTALLATION • Ceiling Covering

Installer _____
Date _____ Cost $ _____

Notes

_____
_____
_____
_____
_____
_____
_____
_____
_____
_____
_____
_____
_____
_____
_____
_____

Tip: Duct tape . . .
need we say more?

_____
_____
_____

53

BATHROOM 3

Notes

WALL COVERING

MEASUREMENTS • Walls

North: Width _____ X Height _____ = _____ sq. ft.

South: Width _____ X Height _____ = _____ sq. ft.

East: Width _____ X Height _____ = _____ sq. ft.

West: Width _____ X Height _____ = _____ sq. ft.

▶ **TYPE & MATERIAL** • First Wall Covering

Description *(paint, paper, paneling, etc.)* _____

Brand & pattern _____

Color & number _____

PURCHASE • First Wall Covering

Retailer _____

Date _____ Cost/unit $ _____

No. of units _____ Total cost $ _____

Warranty _____

INSTALLATION • First Wall Covering

Installer _____

Date _____ Cost $ _____

CLEANING & REFINISHING • First Wall Covering

Company _____

Date _____ Cost $ _____

Company _____

Date _____ Cost $ _____

▶ **TYPE & MATERIAL** • Second Wall Covering

Description *(paint, paper, paneling, etc.)* _____

Brand & pattern _____

Color & number _____

PURCHASE • Second Wall Covering

Retailer _____

Date _____ Cost/unit $ _____

No. of units _____ Total cost $ _____

Warranty _____

INSTALLATION • Second Wall Covering

Installer _____

Date _____ Cost $ _____

CLEANING & REFINISHING • Second Wall Covering

Company _____

Date _____ Cost $ _____

Company _____

Date _____ Cost $ _____

WINDOWS

MEASUREMENTS • Windows

Window 1: Width _____ Height _____
Window 2: Width _____ Height _____

TYPE & MATERIAL • Windows

Description *(vinyl casement, etc.)* _____
Brand & model _____

PURCHASE • Windows

Retailer _____
Date _____ Cost/unit $ _____
No. of units _____ Total cost $ _____
Warranty _____

INSTALLATION • Windows

Installer _____
Date _____ Cost $ _____

WINDOW TREATMENTS

MEASUREMENTS • Window Treatments

Treatment 1: Width _____ X Height _____ = _____ sq. ft.
Treatment 2: Width _____ X Height _____ = _____ sq. ft.

TYPE & MATERIAL • Window Treatments

Description *(draperies, blinds, etc.)* _____
  Brand & model _____
  Color & number _____
Description *(draperies, blinds, etc.)* _____
  Brand & model _____
  Color & number _____

PURCHASE • Window Treatments

Retailer _____
Date _____ Cost/unit $ _____
No. of units _____ Total cost $ _____
Warranty _____

INSTALLATION • Window Treatments

Installer _____
Date _____ Cost $ _____

CLEANING & REFINISHING • Window Treatments

Company _____
  Date _____ Cost $ _____
Company _____
  Date _____ Cost $ _____

Notes

_____

Tip: Don't throw out those old, hardened paint brushes. Instead, you can soak them in hot vinegar, then wash them with soap and water. To prevent hardening, care for your brushes by rinsing them with a small amount of fabric softener after they are cleaned.

55

BATHROOM 3

Notes

_____
_____
_____
_____
_____
_____
_____
_____
_____
_____
_____
_____
_____
_____
_____
_____
_____
_____
_____
_____
_____
_____
_____
_____
_____
_____
_____
_____

DOOR

MEASUREMENTS • Door
Width _____ Height _____

TYPE & MATERIAL • Door
Description *(oak, masonite, etc.)* _____
Brand & style _____
Color & number _____
Hardware description _____

PURCHASE • Door
Retailer _____
Date _____ Cost/unit $ _____
No. of units _____ Total cost $ _____
Warranty _____

INSTALLATION • Door
Installer _____
Date _____ Cost $ _____

CLEANING & REFINISHING • Door
Company _____
Date _____ Cost $ _____

SAMPLES

Attach Swatch or Daub Paint Here

FIXTURES

CLOSETS

DIAGRAMS/EXTRA NOTES

> *"Home" is any four walls that enclose the right person.*
>
> —Helen Rowland

ENTRY

✏ Notes

_____

_____

_____

_____

_____

_____

_____

_____

_____

_____

_____

_____

_____

_____

_____

_____

_____

_____

_____

_____

_____

_____

_____

_____

FLOOR COVERING

MEASUREMENTS • Floor

Width _____ X Depth _____ = _____ sq. ft.

TYPE & MATERIAL • Floor Covering

Description *(nylon carpet, ceramic tile, etc.)* _____

Brand & pattern _____

Color & number _____

Backing type _____ Pad type _____

PURCHASE • Floor Covering

Retailer _____

Date _____ Cost/unit $ _____

No. of units _____ Total cost $ _____

Warranty _____

INSTALLATION • Floor Covering

Installer _____

Date _____ Cost $ _____

CLEANING & REFINISHING • Floor Covering

Company _____

Date _____ Cost $ _____

Company _____

Date _____ Cost $ _____

CEILING COVERING

TYPE & MATERIAL • Ceiling Covering

Description *(paint, spray texture, etc.)* _____

Brand & pattern _____

Color & number _____

PURCHASE • Ceiling Covering

Retailer _____

Date _____ Cost/unit $ _____

No. of units _____ Total cost $ _____

Warranty _____

INSTALLATION • Ceiling Covering

Installer _____

Date _____ Cost $ _____

WALL COVERING

MEASUREMENTS • Walls

North: Width _____ X Height _____ = _____ sq. ft.
South: Width _____ X Height _____ = _____ sq. ft.
East: Width _____ X Height _____ = _____ sq. ft.
West: Width _____ X Height _____ = _____ sq. ft.

▶ **TYPE & MATERIAL** • First Wall Covering
Description *(paint, paper, paneling, etc.)* _____
Brand & pattern _____
Color & number _____

PURCHASE • First Wall Covering
Retailer _____
Date _____ Cost/unit $ _____
No. of units _____ Total cost $ _____
Warranty _____

INSTALLATION • First Wall Covering
Installer _____
Date _____ Cost $ _____

CLEANING & REFINISHING • First Wall Covering
Company _____
Date _____ Cost $ _____
Company _____
Date _____ Cost $ _____

▶ **TYPE & MATERIAL** • Second Wall Covering
Description *(paint, paper, paneling, etc.)* _____
Brand & pattern _____
Color & number _____

PURCHASE • Second Wall Covering
Retailer _____
Date _____ Cost/unit $ _____
No. of units _____ Total cost $ _____
Warranty _____

INSTALLATION • Second Wall Covering
Installer _____
Date _____ Cost $ _____

CLEANING & REFINISHING • Second Wall Covering
Company _____
Date _____ Cost $ _____
Company _____
Date _____ Cost $ _____

Notes

_____
_____
_____
_____
_____
_____
_____
_____
_____
_____
_____
_____
_____
_____
_____
_____
_____
_____
_____
_____
_____

HOW TO

MEASURE A FLOOR
Measure the widest and the longest part of the room. Multiply the width by length to obtain the square feet of the room. You will provide this square foot measurement when purchasing floor covering that comes on a roll, such as carpet and vinyl.

Notes

_____
_____
_____
_____
_____
_____
_____
_____
_____
_____
_____
_____
_____
_____
_____
_____
_____
_____
_____
_____
_____
_____
_____

WINDOWS

MEASUREMENTS • Windows

Window 1: Width _____ Height _____
Window 2: Width _____ Height _____

TYPE & MATERIAL • Windows

Description *(vinyl casement, etc.)* _____
Brand & model _____

PURCHASE • Windows

Retailer _____
Date _____ Cost/unit $ _____
No. of units _____ Total cost $ _____
Warranty _____

INSTALLATION • Windows

Installer _____
Date _____ Cost $ _____

WINDOW TREATMENTS

MEASUREMENTS • Window Treatments

Treatment 1: Width _____ X Height _____ = _____ sq. ft.
Treatment 2: Width _____ X Height _____ = _____ sq. ft.

TYPE & MATERIAL • Window Treatments

Description *(draperies, blinds, etc.)* _____
Brand & model _____
Color & number _____
Description *(draperies, blinds, etc.)* _____
Brand & model _____
Color & number _____

PURCHASE • Window Treatments

Retailer _____
Date _____ Cost/unit $ _____
No. of units _____ Total cost $ _____
Warranty _____

INSTALLATION • Window Treatments

Installer _____
Date _____ Cost $ _____

CLEANING & REFINISHING • Window Treatments

Company _____
Date _____ Cost $ _____
Company _____
Date _____ Cost $ _____

DOORS

MEASUREMENTS • Doors

First Door: Second Door:

Width _____ Height _____   Width _____ Height _____

▶ TYPE & MATERIAL • First Door

Description *(oak, masonite, etc.)* _____
Brand & style _____
Color & number _____
Hardware description _____

PURCHASE • First Door

Retailer _____
Date _____   Cost/unit $ _____
No. of units _____ Total cost $ _____
Warranty _____

INSTALLATION • First Door

Installer _____
Date _____   Cost $ _____

CLEANING & REFINISHING • First Door

Company _____
    Date _____   Cost $ _____
Company _____
    Date _____   Cost $ _____

▶ TYPE & MATERIAL • Second Door

Description *(oak, masonite, etc.)* _____
Brand & style _____
Color & number _____
Hardware description _____

PURCHASE • Second Door

Retailer _____
Date _____   Cost/unit $ _____
No. of units _____ Total cost $ _____
Warranty _____

INSTALLATION • Second Door

Installer _____
Date _____   Cost $ _____

CLEANING & REFINISHING • Second Door

Company _____
    Date _____   Cost $ _____
Company _____
    Date _____   Cost $ _____

Notes

_____
_____
_____
_____
_____
_____
_____
_____
_____
_____
_____
_____
_____
_____
_____
_____
_____
_____
_____
_____
_____
_____

▶ **Tip:** If the nail you need to use is too small to hold while hammering, hold it with a bobby pin.

61

ENTRY

✏ Notes

SAMPLES

Attach Swatch or Daub Paint Here

CLOSETS

DIAGRAMS / EXTRA NOTES

HALL/STAIRS 1

FLOOR COVERING

MEASUREMENTS • Floor
Width _____ X Depth _____ = _____ sq. ft.

TYPE & MATERIAL • Floor Covering
Description *(nylon carpet, ceramic tile, etc.)* _____
Brand & pattern _____
Color & number _____
Backing type _____ Pad type _____

PURCHASE • Floor Covering
Retailer _____
Date _____ Cost/unit $ _____
No. of units _____ Total cost $ _____
Warranty _____

INSTALLATION • Floor Covering
Installer _____
Date _____ Cost $ _____

CLEANING & REFINISHING • Floor Covering
Company _____
    Date _____ Cost $ _____
Company _____
    Date _____ Cost $ _____

CEILING COVERING

TYPE & MATERIAL • Ceiling Covering
Description *(paint, spray texture, etc.)* _____
Brand & pattern _____
Color & number _____

PURCHASE • Ceiling Covering
Retailer _____
Date _____ Cost/unit $ _____
No. of units _____ Total cost $ _____
Warranty _____

INSTALLATION • Ceiling Covering
Installer _____
Date _____ Cost $ _____

Notes
_____
_____
_____
_____
_____
_____
_____
_____
_____
_____
_____
_____
_____
_____
_____
_____
_____
_____

▶ **Tip:** Lighter fluid or vegetable oil will remove old duct tape residue.

63

✏ Notes

WALL COVERING

MEASUREMENTS • Walls

North:	Width _____	X Height _____	= _____ sq. ft.
South:	Width _____	X Height _____	= _____ sq. ft.
East:	Width _____	X Height _____	= _____ sq. ft.
West:	Width _____	X Height _____	= _____ sq. ft.

▶ **TYPE & MATERIAL** • First Wall Covering

Description *(paint, paper, paneling, etc.)* _____
Brand & pattern _____
Color & number _____

PURCHASE • First Wall Covering

Retailer _____
Date _____ Cost/unit $ _____
No. of units _____ Total cost $ _____
Warranty _____

INSTALLATION • First Wall Covering

Installer _____
Date _____ Cost $ _____

CLEANING & REFINISHING • First Wall Covering

Company _____
   Date _____ Cost $ _____
Company _____
   Date _____ Cost $ _____

▶ **TYPE & MATERIAL** • Second Wall Covering

Description *(paint, paper, paneling, etc.)* _____
Brand & pattern _____
Color & number _____

PURCHASE • Second Wall Covering

Retailer _____
Date _____ Cost/unit $ _____
No. of units _____ Total cost $ _____
Warranty _____

INSTALLATION • Second Wall Covering

Installer _____
Date _____ Cost $ _____

CLEANING & REFINISHING • Second Wall Covering

Company _____
   Date _____ Cost $ _____
Company _____
   Date _____ Cost $ _____

WINDOWS

MEASUREMENTS • Windows

Window 1: Width _____ Height _____
Window 2: Width _____ Height _____

TYPE & MATERIAL • Windows

Description *(vinyl casement, etc.)* _____
Brand & model _____

PURCHASE • Windows

Retailer _____
Date _____ Cost/unit $ _____
No. of units _____ Total cost $ _____
Warranty _____

INSTALLATION • Windows

Installer _____
Date _____ Cost $ _____

WINDOW TREATMENTS

MEASUREMENTS • Window Treatments

Treatment 1: Width _____ X Height _____ = _____ sq. ft.
Treatment 2: Width _____ X Height _____ = _____ sq. ft.

TYPE & MATERIAL • Window Treatments

Description *(draperies, blinds, etc.)* _____
 Brand & model _____
 Color & number _____
Description *(draperies, blinds, etc.)* _____
 Brand & model _____
 Color & number _____

PURCHASE • Window Treatments

Retailer _____
Date _____ Cost/unit $ _____
No. of units _____ Total cost $ _____
Warranty _____

INSTALLATION • Window Treatments

Installer _____
Date _____ Cost $ _____

CLEANING & REFINISHING • Window Treatments

Company _____
 Date _____ Cost $ _____
Company _____
 Date _____ Cost $ _____

Notes

_____
_____
_____
_____
_____
_____
_____
_____
_____
_____
_____
_____
_____
_____
_____
_____
_____
_____
_____

Tip: Before hanging your wallpaper, check each roll for pattern and dye or lot numbers to make sure they are all the same on each bolt. Save labels and packaging in case you need to buy more.

_____
_____

HALL/STAIRS 1

✎ Notes

_____
_____
_____
_____
_____
_____
_____
_____
_____
_____
_____
_____
_____
_____
_____
_____
_____
_____
_____
_____
_____
_____
_____
_____
_____
_____
_____
_____
_____

66

DOOR

MEASUREMENTS • Door
Width _____ Height _____

TYPE & MATERIAL • Door
Description *(oak, masonite, etc.)* _____
Brand & style _____
Color & number _____
Hardware description _____

PURCHASE • Door
Retailer _____
Date _____ Cost/unit $ _____
No. of units _____ Total cost $ _____
Warranty _____

INSTALLATION • Door
Installer _____
Date _____ Cost $ _____

CLEANING & REFINISHING • Door
Company _____
Date _____ Cost $ _____

SAMPLES

Attach Swatch or Daub Paint Here

CLOSETS

_____
_____
_____
_____
_____
_____
_____
_____

HALL/STAIRS 2

FLOOR COVERING

MEASUREMENTS • Floor
Width _____ X Depth _____ = _____ sq. ft.

TYPE & MATERIAL • Floor Covering
Description *(nylon carpet, ceramic tile, etc.)* _____
Brand & pattern _____
Color & number _____
Backing type _____ Pad type _____

PURCHASE • Floor Covering
Retailer _____
Date _____ Cost/unit $ _____
No. of units _____ Total cost $ _____
Warranty _____

INSTALLATION • Floor Covering
Installer _____
Date _____ Cost $ _____

CLEANING & REFINISHING • Floor Covering
Company _____
Date _____ Cost $ _____
Company _____
Date _____ Cost $ _____

CEILING COVERING

TYPE & MATERIAL • Ceiling Covering
Description *(paint, spray texture, etc.)* _____
Brand & pattern _____
Color & number _____

PURCHASE • Ceiling Covering
Retailer _____
Date _____ Cost/unit $ _____
No. of units _____ Total cost $ _____
Warranty _____

INSTALLATION • Ceiling Covering
Installer _____
Date _____ Cost $ _____

Notes
_____
_____
_____
_____
_____
_____
_____
_____
_____
_____
_____
_____
_____
_____
_____

 Tip: Here's how to make your own window cleaner: put 1/3 cup vinegar and 1/4 cup alcohol in a 32 oz. spray bottle, then fill the rest with water. Nothing else is needed.

_____
_____
67
_____

Notes

WALL COVERING

MEASUREMENTS • Walls

North:	Width _____	X Height _____	= _____ sq. ft.
South:	Width _____	X Height _____	= _____ sq. ft.
East:	Width _____	X Height _____	= _____ sq. ft.
West:	Width _____	X Height _____	= _____ sq. ft.

▶ **TYPE & MATERIAL** • First Wall Covering

Description *(paint, paper, paneling, etc.)* _____
Brand & pattern _____
Color & number _____

PURCHASE • First Wall Covering

Retailer _____
Date _____ Cost/unit $ _____
No. of units _____ Total cost $ _____
Warranty _____

INSTALLATION • First Wall Covering

Installer _____
Date _____ Cost $ _____

CLEANING & REFINISHING • First Wall Covering

Company _____
Date _____ Cost $ _____
Company _____
Date _____ Cost $ _____

▶ **TYPE & MATERIAL** • Second Wall Covering

Description *(paint, paper, paneling, etc.)* _____
Brand & pattern _____
Color & number _____

PURCHASE • Second Wall Covering

Retailer _____
Date _____ Cost/unit $ _____
No. of units _____ Total cost $ _____
Warranty _____

INSTALLATION • Second Wall Covering

Installer _____
Date _____ Cost $ _____

CLEANING & REFINISHING • Second Wall Covering

Company _____
Date _____ Cost $ _____
Company _____
Date _____ Cost $ _____

WINDOWS

MEASUREMENTS • Windows

Window 1: Width _____ Height _____

Window 2: Width _____ Height _____

TYPE & MATERIAL • Windows

Description *(vinyl casement, etc.)* _____

Brand & model _____

PURCHASE • Windows

Retailer _____

Date _____ Cost/unit $ _____

No. of units _____ Total cost $ _____

Warranty _____

INSTALLATION • Windows

Installer _____

Date _____ Cost $ _____

WINDOW TREATMENTS

MEASUREMENTS • Window Treatments

Treatment 1: Width _____ X Height _____ = _____ sq. ft.

Treatment 2: Width _____ X Height _____ = _____ sq. ft.

TYPE & MATERIAL • Window Treatments

Description *(draperies, blinds, etc.)* _____

Brand & model _____

Color & number _____

Description *(draperies, blinds, etc.)* _____

Brand & model _____

Color & number _____

PURCHASE • Window Treatments

Retailer _____

Date _____ Cost/unit $ _____

No. of units _____ Total cost $ _____

Warranty _____

INSTALLATION • Window Treatments

Installer _____

Date _____ Cost $ _____

CLEANING & REFINISHING • Window Treatments

Company _____

Date _____ Cost $ _____

Company _____

Date _____ Cost $ _____

Notes

_____
_____
_____
_____
_____
_____
_____
_____
_____
_____
_____
_____
_____
_____
_____
_____
_____
_____
_____
_____

Tip: Keep accurate records about your home. It will prove to be a valuable asset when trying to sell.

✎ **Notes**

DOOR

MEASUREMENTS • Door
Width _____ Height _____

TYPE & MATERIAL • Door
Description *(oak, masonite, etc.)* _____
Brand & style _____
Color & number _____
Hardware description _____

PURCHASE • Door
Retailer _____
Date _____ Cost/unit $ _____
No. of units _____ Total cost $ _____
Warranty _____

INSTALLATION • Door
Installer _____
Date _____ Cost $ _____

CLEANING & REFINISHING • Door
Company _____
Date _____ Cost $ _____

SAMPLES

Attach Swatch or Daub Paint Here

CLOSETS

HALL/STAIRS 3

FLOOR COVERING

MEASUREMENTS • Floor
Width _____ X Depth _____ = _____ sq. ft.

TYPE & MATERIAL • Floor Covering
Description *(nylon carpet, ceramic tile, etc.)* _____
Brand & pattern _____
Color & number _____
Backing type _____ Pad type _____

PURCHASE • Floor Covering
Retailer _____
Date _____ Cost/unit $ _____
No. of units _____ Total cost $ _____
Warranty _____

INSTALLATION • Floor Covering
Installer _____
Date _____ Cost $ _____

CLEANING & REFINISHING • Floor Covering
Company _____
Date _____ Cost $ _____
Company _____
Date _____ Cost $ _____

CEILING COVERING

TYPE & MATERIAL • Ceiling Covering
Description *(paint, spray texture, etc.)* _____
Brand & pattern _____
Color & number _____

PURCHASE • Ceiling Covering
Retailer _____
Date _____ Cost/unit $ _____
No. of units _____ Total cost $ _____
Warranty _____

INSTALLATION • Ceiling Covering
Installer _____
Date _____ Cost $ _____

Notes
_____
_____
_____
_____
_____
_____
_____
_____
_____
_____
_____
_____
_____
_____

▶ **Tip:** You can use a cotton ball dipped in rubbing alcohol to wipe dust off of candles.

_____
_____

HALL/STAIRS 3

_____
_____
_____
_____
_____
_____
_____
_____
_____
_____
_____
_____
_____
_____
_____
_____
_____
_____
_____
_____
_____
_____
_____
_____
_____

WALL COVERING

MEASUREMENTS • Walls

North: Width _____ X Height _____ = _____ sq. ft.
South: Width _____ X Height _____ = _____ sq. ft.
East: Width _____ X Height _____ = _____ sq. ft.
West: Width _____ X Height _____ = _____ sq. ft.

▶ **TYPE & MATERIAL** • First Wall Covering
Description *(paint, paper, paneling, etc.)* _____
Brand & pattern _____
Color & number _____

PURCHASE • First Wall Covering
Retailer _____
Date _____ Cost/unit $ _____
No. of units _____ Total cost $ _____
Warranty _____

INSTALLATION • First Wall Covering
Installer _____
Date _____ Cost $ _____

CLEANING & REFINISHING • First Wall Covering
Company _____
  Date _____ Cost $ _____
Company _____
  Date _____ Cost $ _____

▶ **TYPE & MATERIAL** • Second Wall Covering
Description *(paint, paper, paneling, etc.)* _____
Brand & pattern _____
Color & number _____

PURCHASE • Second Wall Covering
Retailer _____
Date _____ Cost/unit $ _____
No. of units _____ Total cost $ _____
Warranty _____

INSTALLATION • Second Wall Covering
Installer _____
Date _____ Cost $ _____

CLEANING & REFINISHING • Second Wall Covering
Company _____
  Date _____ Cost $ _____
Company _____
  Date _____ Cost $ _____

WINDOWS

MEASUREMENTS • Windows

Window 1: Width _____ Height _____

Window 2: Width _____ Height _____

TYPE & MATERIAL • Windows

Description *(vinyl casement, etc.)* _____

Brand & model _____

PURCHASE • Windows

Retailer _____

Date _____ Cost/unit $ _____

No. of units _____ Total cost $ _____

Warranty _____

INSTALLATION • Windows

Installer _____

Date _____ Cost $ _____

WINDOW TREATMENTS

MEASUREMENTS • Window Treatments

Treatment 1: Width _____ X Height _____ = _____ sq. ft.

Treatment 2: Width _____ X Height _____ = _____ sq. ft.

TYPE & MATERIAL • Window Treatments

Description *(draperies, blinds, etc.)* _____

Brand & model _____

Color & number _____

Description *(draperies, blinds, etc.)* _____

Brand & model _____

Color & number _____

PURCHASE • Window Treatments

Retailer _____

Date _____ Cost/unit $ _____

No. of units _____ Total cost $ _____

Warranty _____

INSTALLATION • Window Treatments

Installer _____

Date _____ Cost $ _____

CLEANING & REFINISHING • Window Treatments

Company _____

Date _____ Cost $ _____

Company _____

Date _____ Cost $ _____

Notes

_____

Tip: Each time you look up a number in the phone book, highlight it. It will be quicker the next time around!

73

HALL/STAIRS 3

![pencil] Notes

_____
_____
_____
_____
_____
_____
_____
_____
_____
_____
_____
_____
_____
_____
_____
_____
_____
_____
_____
_____
_____
_____
_____
_____
_____
_____
_____

DOOR

MEASUREMENTS • Door
Width _____ Height _____

TYPE & MATERIAL • Door
Description *(oak, masonite, etc.)* _____
Brand & style _____
Color & number _____
Hardware description _____

PURCHASE • Door
Retailer _____
Date _____ Cost/unit $ _____
No. of units _____ Total cost $ _____
Warranty _____

INSTALLATION • Door
Installer _____
Date _____ Cost $ _____

CLEANING & REFINISHING • Door
Company _____
Date _____ Cost $ _____

SAMPLES

Attach Swatch or Daub Paint Here

CLOSETS

_____
_____
_____
_____
_____
_____
_____

MISCELLANEOUS
ROOM 1

FLOOR COVERING

MEASUREMENTS • Floor

Width _____ X Depth _____ = _____ sq. ft.

TYPE & MATERIAL • Floor Covering

Description *(nylon carpet, ceramic tile, etc.)* _____
Brand & pattern _____
Color & number _____
Backing type _____ Pad type _____

PURCHASE • Floor Covering

Retailer _____
Date _____ Cost/unit $ _____
No. of units _____ Total cost $ _____
Warranty _____

INSTALLATION • Floor Covering

Installer _____
Date _____ Cost $ _____

CLEANING & REFINISHING • Floor Covering

Company _____
   Date _____ Cost $ _____
Company _____
   Date _____ Cost $ _____

CEILING COVERING

TYPE & MATERIAL • Ceiling Covering

Description *(paint, spray texture, etc.)* _____
Brand & pattern _____
Color & number _____

PURCHASE • Ceiling Covering

Retailer _____
Date _____ Cost/unit $ _____
No. of units _____ Total cost $ _____
Warranty _____

INSTALLATION • Ceiling Covering

Installer _____
Date _____ Cost $ _____

Notes

_____
_____
_____
_____
_____
_____
_____
_____
_____
_____
_____
_____
_____
_____

The home should be the treasure chest of living.

—Le Corbusier

_____
_____

75

_____
_____

✏️ Notes

MEASUREMENTS • Walls

North: Width _____	X Height _____	= _____	sq. ft.
South: Width _____	X Height _____	= _____	sq. ft.
East: Width _____	X Height _____	= _____	sq. ft.
West: Width _____	X Height _____	= _____	sq. ft.

▶ **TYPE & MATERIAL** • First Wall Covering
Description *(paint, paper, paneling, etc.)* _____
Brand & pattern _____
Color & number _____

PURCHASE • First Wall Covering
Retailer _____
Date _____ Cost/unit $ _____
No. of units _____ Total cost $ _____
Warranty _____

INSTALLATION • First Wall Covering
Installer _____
Date _____ Cost $ _____

CLEANING & REFINISHING • First Wall Covering
Company _____
  Date _____ Cost $ _____
Company _____
  Date _____ Cost $ _____

▶ **TYPE & MATERIAL** • Second Wall Covering
Description *(paint, paper, paneling, etc.)* _____
Brand & pattern _____
Color & number _____

PURCHASE • Second Wall Covering
Retailer _____
Date _____ Cost/unit $ _____
No. of units _____ Total cost $ _____
Warranty _____

INSTALLATION • Second Wall Covering
Installer _____
Date _____ Cost $ _____

CLEANING & REFINISHING • Second Wall Covering
Company _____
  Date _____ Cost $ _____
Company _____
  Date _____ Cost $ _____

WINDOWS

MEASUREMENTS • Windows
Window 1: Width _____ Height _____
Window 2: Width _____ Height _____

TYPE & MATERIAL • Windows
Description *(vinyl casement, etc.)* _____
Brand & model _____

PURCHASE • Windows
Retailer _____
Date _____ Cost/unit $ _____
No. of units _____ Total cost $ _____
Warranty _____

INSTALLATION • Windows
Installer _____
Date _____ Cost $ _____

WINDOW TREATMENTS

MEASUREMENTS • Window Treatments
Treatment 1: Width _____ X Height _____ = _____ sq. ft.
Treatment 2: Width _____ X Height _____ = _____ sq. ft.

TYPE & MATERIAL • Window Treatments
Description *(draperies, blinds, etc.)* _____
Brand & model _____
Color & number _____
Description *(draperies, blinds, etc.)* _____
Brand & model _____
Color & number _____

PURCHASE • Window Treatments
Retailer _____
Date _____ Cost/unit $ _____
No. of units _____ Total cost $ _____
Warranty _____

INSTALLATION • Window Treatments
Installer _____
Date _____ Cost $ _____

CLEANING & REFINISHING • Window Treatments
Company _____
Date _____ Cost $ _____
Company _____
Date _____ Cost $ _____

Notes
_____

Tip: Have your kids help dust the furniture by wearing an old sock on each hand. Dusting will become fun!

77

Notes

DOOR

MEASUREMENTS • Door
Width _____ Height _____

TYPE & MATERIAL • Door
Description *(oak, masonite, etc.)* _____
Brand & style _____
Color & number _____
Hardware description _____

PURCHASE • Door
Retailer _____
Date _____ Cost/unit $ _____
No. of units _____ Total cost $ _____
Warranty _____

INSTALLATION • Door
Installer _____
Date _____ Cost $ _____

CLEANING & REFINISHING • Door
Company _____
Date _____ Cost $ _____

SAMPLES

Attach Swatch or Daub Paint Here

CLOSETS

MISCELLANEOUS
ROOM 2

FLOOR COVERING

MEASUREMENTS • Floor
Width _____ X Depth _____ = _____ sq. ft.

TYPE & MATERIAL • Floor Covering
Description *(nylon carpet, ceramic tile, etc.)* _____
Brand & pattern _____
Color & number _____
Backing type _____ Pad type _____

PURCHASE • Floor Covering
Retailer _____
Date _____ Cost/unit $ _____
No. of units _____ Total cost $ _____
Warranty _____

INSTALLATION • Floor Covering
Installer _____
Date _____ Cost $ _____

CLEANING & REFINISHING • Floor Covering
Company _____
Date _____ Cost $ _____
Company _____
Date _____ Cost $ _____

CEILING COVERING

TYPE & MATERIAL • Ceiling Covering
Description *(paint, spray texture, etc.)* _____
Brand & pattern _____
Color & number _____

PURCHASE • Ceiling Covering
Retailer _____
Date _____ Cost/unit $ _____
No. of units _____ Total cost $ _____
Warranty _____

INSTALLATION • Ceiling Covering
Installer _____
Date _____ Cost $ _____

Notes
_____
_____
_____
_____
_____
_____
_____
_____
_____
_____
_____
_____
_____
_____
_____

*Human beings are
the only creatures on
earth that allow their
children to come back
home.*

—Bill Cosby

79

Notes

WALL COVERING

MEASUREMENTS • Walls

North: Width _____ X Height _____ = _____ sq. ft.
South: Width _____ X Height _____ = _____ sq. ft.
East: Width _____ X Height _____ = _____ sq. ft.
West: Width _____ X Height _____ = _____ sq. ft.

▶ **TYPE & MATERIAL** • First Wall Covering
Description *(paint, paper, paneling, etc.)* _____
Brand & pattern _____
Color & number _____

PURCHASE • First Wall Covering
Retailer _____
Date _____ Cost/unit $ _____
No. of units _____ Total cost $ _____
Warranty _____

INSTALLATION • First Wall Covering
Installer _____
Date _____ Cost $ _____

CLEANING & REFINISHING • First Wall Covering
Company _____
Date _____ Cost $ _____
Company _____
Date _____ Cost $ _____

▶ **TYPE & MATERIAL** • Second Wall Covering
Description *(paint, paper, paneling, etc.)* _____
Brand & pattern _____
Color & number _____

PURCHASE • Second Wall Covering
Retailer _____
Date _____ Cost/unit $ _____
No. of units _____ Total cost $ _____
Warranty _____

INSTALLATION • Second Wall Covering
Installer _____
Date _____ Cost $ _____

CLEANING & REFINISHING • Second Wall Covering
Company _____
Date _____ Cost $ _____
Company _____
Date _____ Cost $ _____

WINDOWS

MEASUREMENTS • Windows

Window 1: Width _____ Height _____

Window 2: Width _____ Height _____

TYPE & MATERIAL • Windows

Description *(vinyl casement, etc.)* _____

Brand & model _____

PURCHASE • Windows

Retailer _____

Date _____ Cost/unit $ _____

No. of units _____ Total cost $ _____

Warranty _____

INSTALLATION • Windows

Installer _____

Date _____ Cost $ _____

WINDOW TREATMENTS

MEASUREMENTS • Window Treatments

Treatment 1: Width _____ X Height _____ = _____ sq. ft.

Treatment 2: Width _____ X Height _____ = _____ sq. ft.

TYPE & MATERIAL • Window Treatments

Description *(draperies, blinds, etc.)* _____

 Brand & model _____

 Color & number _____

Description *(draperies, blinds, etc.)* _____

 Brand & model _____

 Color & number _____

PURCHASE • Window Treatments

Retailer _____

Date _____ Cost/unit $ _____

No. of units _____ Total cost $ _____

Warranty _____

INSTALLATION • Window Treatments

Installer _____

Date _____ Cost $ _____

CLEANING & REFINISHING • Window Treatments

Company _____

 Date _____ Cost $ _____

Company _____

 Date _____ Cost $ _____

Notes

_____

Tip: Start a "decorating ideas" notebook. Cut out pictures of rooms or items that catch your eye. After you have accumulated a few, you will begin to see a pattern of the decorating style that is right for you.

81

MISCELLANEOUS
ROOM 2

✏️ Notes

DOOR

MEASUREMENTS • Door
  Width _____ Height _____

TYPE & MATERIAL • Door
  Description *(oak, masonite, etc.)* _____
  Brand & style _____
  Color & number _____
  Hardware description _____

PURCHASE • Door
  Retailer _____
  Date _____ Cost/unit $ _____
  No. of units _____ Total cost $ _____
  Warranty _____

INSTALLATION • Door
  Installer _____
  Date _____ Cost $ _____

CLEANING & REFINISHING • Door
  Company _____
  Date _____ Cost $ _____

SAMPLES

Attach Swatch or Daub Paint Here

CLOSETS

MISCELLANEOUS
ROOM 3

FLOOR COVERING

MEASUREMENTS • Floor

Width _____ X Depth _____ = _____ sq. ft.

TYPE & MATERIAL • Floor Covering

Description *(nylon carpet, ceramic tile, etc.)* _____

Brand & pattern _____

Color & number _____

Backing type _____ Pad type _____

PURCHASE • Floor Covering

Retailer _____

Date _____ Cost/unit $ _____

No. of units _____ Total cost $ _____

Warranty _____

INSTALLATION • Floor Covering

Installer _____

Date _____ Cost $ _____

CLEANING & REFINISHING • Floor Covering

Company _____

Date _____ Cost $ _____

Company _____

Date _____ Cost $ _____

CEILING COVERING

TYPE & MATERIAL • Ceiling Covering

Description *(paint, spray texture, etc.)* _____

Brand & pattern _____

Color & number _____

PURCHASE • Ceiling Covering

Retailer _____

Date _____ Cost/unit $ _____

No. of units _____ Total cost $ _____

Warranty _____

INSTALLATION • Ceiling Covering

Installer _____

Date _____ Cost $ _____

Notes

_____
_____
_____
_____
_____
_____
_____
_____
_____
_____
_____
_____
_____
_____
_____

Be it ever so humble, there's no place like home.

—J. Howard Payne

✏️ Notes

WALL COVERING

MEASUREMENTS • Walls

North:	Width _____	X Height _____	= _____	sq. ft.
South:	Width _____	X Height _____	= _____	sq. ft.
East:	Width _____	X Height _____	= _____	sq. ft.
West:	Width _____	X Height _____	= _____	sq. ft.

▶ **TYPE & MATERIAL** • First Wall Covering

Description *(paint, paper, paneling, etc.)* _____

Brand & pattern _____

Color & number _____

PURCHASE • First Wall Covering

Retailer _____

Date _____ Cost/unit $ _____

No. of units _____ Total cost $ _____

Warranty _____

INSTALLATION • First Wall Covering

Installer _____

Date _____ Cost $ _____

CLEANING & REFINISHING • First Wall Covering

Company _____

Date _____ Cost $ _____

Company _____

Date _____ Cost $ _____

▶ **TYPE & MATERIAL** • Second Wall Covering

Description *(paint, paper, paneling, etc.)* _____

Brand & pattern _____

Color & number _____

PURCHASE • Second Wall Covering

Retailer _____

Date _____ Cost/unit $ _____

No. of units _____ Total cost $ _____

Warranty _____

INSTALLATION • Second Wall Covering

Installer _____

Date _____ Cost $ _____

CLEANING & REFINISHING • Second Wall Covering

Company _____

Date _____ Cost $ _____

Company _____

Date _____ Cost $ _____

WINDOWS

MEASUREMENTS • Windows

    Window 1: Width _____ Height _____

    Window 2: Width _____ Height _____

TYPE & MATERIAL • Windows

    Description *(vinyl casement, etc.)* _____

    Brand & model _____

PURCHASE • Windows

    Retailer _____

    Date _____ Cost/unit $ _____

    No. of units _____ Total cost $ _____

    Warranty _____

INSTALLATION • Windows

    Installer _____

    Date _____ Cost $ _____

WINDOW TREATMENTS

MEASUREMENTS • Window Treatments

    Treatment 1: Width _____ X Height _____ = _____ sq. ft.

    Treatment 2: Width _____ X Height _____ = _____ sq. ft.

TYPE & MATERIAL • Window Treatments

    Description *(draperies, blinds, etc.)* _____

      Brand & model _____

      Color & number _____

    Description *(draperies, blinds, etc.)* _____

      Brand & model _____

      Color & number _____

PURCHASE • Window Treatments

    Retailer _____

    Date _____ Cost/unit $ _____

    No. of units _____ Total cost $ _____

    Warranty _____

INSTALLATION • Window Treatments

    Installer _____

    Date _____ Cost $ _____

CLEANING & REFINISHING • Window Treatments

    Company _____

      Date _____ Cost $ _____

    Company _____

      Date _____ Cost $ _____

Notes

_____

_____

_____

_____

_____

_____

_____

_____

_____

_____

_____

_____

_____

_____

_____

_____

If you foolishly ignore beauty, you'll soon find yourself without it. Your life will be impoverished.

—Frank Lloyd Wright

✎ Notes

DOOR

MEASUREMENTS • Door
Width _____ Height _____

TYPE & MATERIAL • Door
Description *(oak, masonite, etc.)* _____
Brand & style _____
Color & number _____
Hardware description _____

PURCHASE • Door
Retailer _____
Date _____ Cost/unit $ _____
No. of units _____ Total cost $ _____
Warranty _____

INSTALLATION • Door
Installer _____
Date _____ Cost $ _____

CLEANING & REFINISHING • Door
Company _____
Date _____ Cost $ _____

SAMPLES

Attach Swatch or Daub Paint Here

CLOSETS

LAUNDRY ROOM

FLOOR COVERING

MEASUREMENTS • Floor
Width _____ X Depth _____ = _____ sq. ft.

TYPE & MATERIAL • Floor Covering
Description *(nylon carpet, ceramic tile, etc.)* _____
Brand & pattern _____
Color & number _____
Backing type _____ Pad type _____

PURCHASE • Floor Covering
Retailer _____
Date _____ Cost/unit $ _____
No. of units _____ Total cost $ _____
Warranty _____

INSTALLATION • Floor Covering
Installer _____
Date _____ Cost $ _____

CLEANING & REFINISHING • Floor Covering
Company _____
Date _____ Cost $ _____
Company _____
Date _____ Cost $ _____

CEILING COVERING

TYPE & MATERIAL • Ceiling Covering
Description *(paint, spray texture, etc.)* _____
Brand & pattern _____
Color & number _____

PURCHASE • Ceiling Covering
Retailer _____
Date _____ Cost/unit $ _____
No. of units _____ Total cost $ _____
Warranty _____

INSTALLATION • Ceiling Covering
Installer _____
Date _____ Cost $ _____

Notes
_____
_____
_____
_____
_____
_____
_____
_____
_____
_____
_____
_____
_____
_____
_____

▶ **Tip:** When replacing cabinets, don't throw the old ones out. They can be used for storage in the basement, laundry room, or garage.

_____
_____
_____

87

LAUNDRY ROOM

WALL COVERING

MEASUREMENTS • Walls

North:	Width _____	X Height _____	= _____ sq. ft.
South:	Width _____	X Height _____	= _____ sq. ft.
East:	Width _____	X Height _____	= _____ sq. ft.
West:	Width _____	X Height _____	= _____ sq. ft.

▶ **TYPE & MATERIAL** • First Wall Covering

Description *(paint, paper, paneling, etc.)* _____
Brand & pattern _____
Color & number _____

PURCHASE • First Wall Covering

Retailer _____
Date _____ Cost/unit $ _____
No. of units _____ Total cost $ _____
Warranty _____

INSTALLATION • First Wall Covering

Installer _____
Date _____ Cost $ _____

CLEANING & REFINISHING • First Wall Covering

Company _____
　　Date _____ Cost $ _____
Company _____
　　Date _____ Cost $ _____

▶ **TYPE & MATERIAL** • Second Wall Covering

Description *(paint, paper, paneling, etc.)* _____
Brand & pattern _____
Color & number _____

PURCHASE • Second Wall Covering

Retailer _____
Date _____ Cost/unit $ _____
No. of units _____ Total cost $ _____
Warranty _____

INSTALLATION • Second Wall Covering

Installer _____
Date _____ Cost $ _____

CLEANING & REFINISHING • Second Wall Covering

Company _____
　　Date _____ Cost $ _____
Company _____
　　Date _____ Cost $ _____

WINDOWS

MEASUREMENTS • Windows

    Window 1: Width _____ Height _____

    Window 2: Width _____ Height _____

TYPE & MATERIAL • Windows

    Description *(vinyl casement, etc.)* _____

    Brand & model _____

PURCHASE • Windows

    Retailer _____

    Date _____ Cost/unit $ _____

    No. of units _____ Total cost $ _____

    Warranty _____

INSTALLATION • Windows

    Installer _____

    Date _____ Cost $ _____

WINDOW TREATMENTS

MEASUREMENTS • Window Treatments

    Treatment 1: Width _____ X Height _____ = _____ sq. ft.

    Treatment 2: Width _____ X Height _____ = _____ sq. ft.

TYPE & MATERIAL • Window Treatments

    Description *(draperies, blinds, etc.)* _____

      Brand & model _____

      Color & number _____

    Description *(draperies, blinds, etc.)* _____

      Brand & model _____

      Color & number _____

PURCHASE • Window Treatments

    Retailer _____

    Date _____ Cost/unit $ _____

    No. of units _____ Total cost $ _____

    Warranty _____

INSTALLATION • Window Treatments

    Installer _____

    Date _____ Cost $ _____

CLEANING & REFINISHING • Window Treatments

    Company _____

      Date _____ Cost $ _____

    Company _____

      Date _____ Cost $ _____

LAUNDRY ROOM

Notes

▶ **Tip:** Start a file for receipts that pertain to household items, warranties, and product information.

LAUNDRY ROOM

✏️ Notes

_____

DOOR

MEASUREMENTS • Door
Width _____ Height _____

TYPE & MATERIAL • Door
Description *(oak, masonite, etc.)* _____
Brand & style _____
Color & number _____
Hardware description _____

PURCHASE • Door
Retailer _____
Date _____ Cost/unit $ _____
No. of units _____ Total cost $ _____
Warranty _____

INSTALLATION • Door
Installer _____
Date _____ Cost $ _____

CLEANING & REFINISHING • Door
Company _____
Date _____ Cost $ _____

APPLIANCES

Type *(washer, dryer, etc.)* _____
Manufacturer _____
Model/Lot no. _____ Serial no. _____
Retailer _____
Date _____ Cost $ _____ Warranty period _____
Authorized service center _____
Maintenance/service _____

Type *(washer, dryer, etc.)* _____
Manufacturer _____
Model/Lot no. _____ Serial no. _____
Retailer _____
Date _____ Cost $ _____ Warranty period _____
Authorized service center _____
Maintenance/service _____

SAMPLES

Attach Swatch or Daub Paint Here

CLOSETS

DIAGRAMS/EXTRA NOTES

Notes

Tip: When choosing color to use in your home, keep in mind the psychology of color. Blue is cool and calming, creating a feeling of space. Red is hot and vibrant, a great color to warm up a room. Green is cool, nurturing, relaxing. Yellow is warm, cheery, and welcoming.

91

GARAGE

FLOOR COVERING

MEASUREMENTS • Floor
Width _____ X Depth _____ = _____ sq. ft.

TYPE & MATERIAL • Floor Covering
Description *(cement, paint, etc.)* _____
Brand & pattern _____
Color & number _____

PURCHASE • Floor Covering
Retailer _____
Date _____ Cost/unit $ _____
No. of units _____ Total cost $ _____
Warranty _____

INSTALLATION • Floor Covering
Installer _____
Date _____ Cost $ _____

CLEANING & REFINISHING • Floor Covering
Company _____
Date _____ Cost $ _____
Company _____
Date _____ Cost $ _____

CEILING COVERING

TYPE & MATERIAL • Ceiling Covering
Description *(paint, spray texture, etc.)* _____
Brand & pattern _____
Color & number _____

PURCHASE • Ceiling Covering
Retailer _____
Date _____ Cost/unit $ _____
No. of units _____ Total cost $ _____
Warranty _____

INSTALLATION • Ceiling Covering
Installer _____
Date _____ Cost $ _____

Notes

WALL COVERING

MEASUREMENTS • Walls

North:	Width ____	X Height ____	= ____	sq. ft.
South:	Width ____	X Height ____	= ____	sq. ft.
East:	Width ____	X Height ____	= ____	sq. ft.
West:	Width ____	X Height ____	= ____	sq. ft.

TYPE & MATERIAL • Wall Covering

Description *(paint, plywood, etc.)* _____

Brand & pattern _____

Color & number _____

PURCHASE • Wall Covering

Retailer _____

Date _____ Cost/unit $ _____

No. of units _____ Total cost $ _____

Warranty _____

INSTALLATION • Wall Covering

Installer _____

Date _____ Cost $ _____

CLEANING & REFINISHING • Wall Covering

Company _____

Date _____ Cost $ _____

Company _____

Date _____ Cost $ _____

DOORS

MEASUREMENTS • Doors

Overhead Door: Second Door:

Width ____ Height ____ Width ____ Height ____

▶ **TYPE & MATERIAL** • Overhead Door

Description *(aluminum, wood, etc.)* _____

Brand & style _____

Color & number _____

Hardware description _____

PURCHASE • Overhead Door

Retailer _____

Date _____ Cost/unit $ _____

No. of units _____ Total cost $ _____

Warranty _____

INSTALLATION • Overhead Door

Installer _____

Date _____ Cost $ _____

Notes

_____
_____
_____
_____
_____
_____
_____
_____
_____
_____
_____
_____
_____
_____
_____
_____
_____
_____
_____
_____
_____
_____

▶ **Tip:** Oil stains on the driveway can be at least partially removed by dumping a generous amount of kitty litter on the stain. Then step on the kitty litter to grind it in. This will absorb the grease.

93

GARAGE

Notes

Doors *(continued)*

CLEANING & REFINISHING • Overhead Door
Company _____
    Date _____ Cost $ _____
Company _____
    Date _____ Cost $ _____

▶ TYPE & MATERIAL • Second Door
Description *(oak, steel, etc.)* _____
Brand & style _____
Color & number _____
Hardware description _____

PURCHASE • Second Door
Retailer _____
Date _____ Cost/unit $ _____
No. of units _____ Total cost $ _____
Warranty _____

INSTALLATION • Second Door
Installer _____
Date _____ Cost $ _____

CLEANING & REFINISHING • Second Door
Company _____
    Date _____ Cost $ _____
Company _____
    Date _____ Cost $ _____

GARAGE DOOR OPENER

TYPE • Garage Door Opener
Description _____
Brand & model _____

PURCHASE • Garage Door Opener
Retailer _____
Date _____ Cost $ _____
Warranty _____

INSTALLATION • Garage Door Opener
Installer _____
Date _____ Cost $ _____

MAINTENANCE • Garage Door Opener
Company _____
    Date _____ Cost $ _____

ROOF

MEASUREMENTS • Roof

Width _____ X Depth _____ = _____ sq. ft.

TYPE & MATERIAL • Roof

Description *(fiberglass shingles, cedar shakes, etc.)* _____
Brand & style _____
Color & number _____
Misc. materials _____ Cost $ _____

PURCHASE • Roof

Retailer _____
Date _____ Cost/unit $ _____
No. of units _____ Total cost $ _____
Warranty _____

INSTALLATION • Roof

Installer _____
Date _____ Cost $ _____

MAINTENANCE • Roof

Company _____
    Date _____ Cost $ _____
Company _____
    Date _____ Cost $ _____

GUTTERS/DOWNSPOUTS

▶ **TYPE & MATERIAL** • Gutters

Description *(steel, vinyl, etc.)* _____
Brand & style _____
Color & number _____

PURCHASE • Gutters

Retailer _____
Date _____ Cost/unit $ _____
No. of units _____ Total cost $ _____
Warranty _____

INSTALLATION • Gutters

Installer _____
Date _____ Cost $ _____

▶ **TYPE & MATERIAL** • Downspouts

Description *(steel, vinyl, etc.)* _____
Brand & style _____
Color & number _____

Notes
_____
_____
_____
_____
_____
_____
_____
_____
_____
_____
_____
_____
_____
_____
_____
_____
_____
_____
_____
_____

▶ **Tip:** Keep gutters and downspouts free of leaves and other debris. Not only will they work better, but you will also save money on maintenance and replacements!

Notes

PURCHASE • Downspouts

Retailer _____

Date _____ Cost/unit $ _____

No. of units _____ Total cost $ _____

Warranty _____

INSTALLATION • Downspouts

Installer _____

Date _____ Cost $ _____

SIDING

▶ **MEASUREMENTS** • First Type of Siding

North: Width _____ X Height _____ = _____ sq. ft.

South: Width _____ X Height _____ = _____ sq. ft.

East: Width _____ X Height _____ = _____ sq. ft.

West: Width _____ X Height _____ = _____ sq. ft.

TYPE & MATERIAL • First Type of Siding

Description *(brick, stucco, etc.)* _____

Brand & style _____

Color & number _____

Type of finish *(paint, stain, etc.)* _____

Brand & number _____

Color & finish _____

PURCHASE • First Type of Siding

Retailer _____

Date _____ Cost/unit $ _____

No. of units _____ Total cost $ _____

Warranty _____

INSTALLATION • First Type of Siding

Installer _____

Date _____ Cost $ _____

CLEANING & REFINISHING • First Type of Siding

Company _____

Date _____ Cost $ _____

Company _____

Date _____ Cost $ _____

▶ **MEASUREMENTS** • Second Type of Siding

North: Width _____ X Height _____ = _____ sq. ft.

South: Width _____ X Height _____ = _____ sq. ft.

East: Width _____ X Height _____ = _____ sq. ft.

West: Width _____ X Height _____ = _____ sq. ft.

Siding *(continued)*

TYPE & MATERIAL • Second Type of Siding
    Description *(brick, stucco, etc.)* _____
        Brand & style _____
        Color & number _____
    Type of finish *(paint, stain, etc.)* _____
        Brand & number _____
        Color & finish _____

PURCHASE • Second Type of Siding
    Retailer _____
    Date _____ Cost/unit $ _____
    No. of units _____ Total cost $ _____
    Warranty _____

INSTALLATION • Second Type of Siding
    Installer _____
    Date _____ Cost $ _____

CLEANING & REFINISHING • Second Type of Siding
    Company _____
    Date _____ Cost $ _____
    Company _____
    Date _____ Cost $ _____

TRIM

▶ **TYPE & MATERIAL** • First Type of Trim
    Description *(wood, vinyl, etc.)* _____
        Brand & style _____
        Color & number _____
    Type of finish *(paint, stain, etc.)* _____
        Brand & number _____
        Color & finish _____

PURCHASE • First Type of Trim
    Retailer _____
    Date _____ Cost/unit $ _____
    No. of units _____ Total cost $ _____
    Warranty _____

INSTALLATION • First Type of Trim
    Installer _____
    Date _____ Cost $ _____

CLEANING & REFINISHING • First Type of Trim
    Company _____
    Date _____ Cost $ _____

Notes

_____

Things are always better at home than a mile away.

—Chinese proverb

GARAGE

Notes

▶ **TYPE & MATERIAL** • Second Type of Trim
    Description *(wood, vinyl, etc.)* _____
      Brand & style _____
      Color & number _____
    Type of finish *(paint, stain, etc.)* _____
      Brand & number _____
      Color & finish _____

PURCHASE • Second Type of Trim
    Retailer _____
    Date _____ Cost/unit $ _____
    No. of units _____ Total cost $ _____
    Warranty _____

INSTALLATION • Second Type of Trim
    Installer _____
    Date _____ Cost $ _____

CLEANING & REFINISHING • Second Type of Trim
    Company _____
      Date _____ Cost $ _____
    Company _____
      Date _____ Cost $ _____

FIXTURES

Notes

Tip: Improvements to the home often increase its value. So which ones pay back?

New heating system: 100%
Remodel kitchen: 90-100%
Add a bathroom: 92%
Add a family room: 86%
Build a deck: 73%
Add swimming pool: 44%
Finish basement: 15%

ADDITIONAL
INFORMATION

COOLING/HEATING

AIR CONDITIONER • Cooling

Type *(electric, natural gas, etc.)*
Manufacturer
Model no. _____ Serial no.
Retailer
Date _____ Cost $
Warranty period _____ Efficiency
Filter type _____ Size
Cleaned/serviced by
    Date _____ Cost $
Cleaned/serviced by
    Date _____ Cost $

FIREPLACE • Heating

Insert Manufacturer
    Model no. _____ Serial no.
    Retailer
    Date _____ Cost $
    Warranty period
    Installed by
    Date _____ Cost $
Chimney cleaned by
    Date _____ Cost $
Chimney cleaned by
    Date _____ Cost $

HEAT EXCHANGER • Heating

Manufacturer
Model no. _____ Serial no.
Retailer
Date _____ Cost $
Warranty period _____ Efficiency
Installed by
    Date _____ Cost $
Cleaned/serviced by
    Date _____ Cost $
Cleaned/serviced by
    Date _____ Cost $

Notes

Cooling/Heating *(continued)*

HEAT PUMP • Heating
    Type *(electric, fuel oil, etc.)* _____
    Manufacturer _____
    Model no. _____ Serial no. _____
    Retailer _____
    Date _____ Cost $ _____
    Warranty period _____ Efficiency _____
    Filter type _____ Size _____
    Cleaned/serviced by _____
        Date _____ Cost $ _____
    Cleaned/serviced by _____
        Date _____ Cost $ _____

HEATING PLANT • Heating
    Type *(electric, fuel oil, etc.)* _____
    Manufacturer _____
    Model no. _____ Serial no. _____
    Retailer/Contractor _____
    Date _____ Cost $ _____
    Warranty period _____ Efficiency _____
    Filter type _____ Size _____
    Cleaned/serviced by _____
        Date _____ Cost $ _____
    Cleaned/serviced by _____
        Date _____ Cost $ _____

WOOD STOVE • Heating
    Manufacturer _____
    Model no. _____ Serial no. _____
    Retailer/Contractor _____
    Date _____ Cost $ _____
    Warranty period _____ Efficiency _____
    Chimney cleaned by _____
        Date _____ Cost $ _____
    Chimney cleaned by _____
        Date _____ Cost $ _____

OTHER HEATING • Heating

_____
_____
_____
_____
_____

Notes

_____

▶ **Tip:** Items needed in a basic tool kit for the interior of your home: Screwdrivers—flat head and phillips head, claw hammer, level, tape measure, utility knife, pliers, and an assortment of nails, picture hooks, and screws.

101

INSULATION

INSULATION

ATTIC • Insulation

    Type *(fiberglass rolls, etc.)* _____

    Manufacturer _____

    Retailer _____

    Date _____ Cost/unit $ _____

    No. of units _____ Total cost $ _____

    R-value added _____ Previous R-value _____

    Aggregate R-value _____ Thickness _____

    Type of vapor barrier *(6 mil poly, etc.)* _____

    Installed by _____

        Date _____ Cost $ _____

WALLS • Insulation

    First type of insulation *(fiberglass rolls, etc.)* _____

        Manufacturer _____

        Retailer _____

        Date _____ Cost/unit $ _____

        No. of units _____ Total cost $ _____

        R-value added _____ Previous R-value _____

        Aggregate R-value _____ Thickness _____

        Type of vapor barrier *(6 mil poly, etc.)* _____

        Installed by _____

        Date _____ Cost $ _____

    Second type of insulation *(fiberglass rolls, etc.)* _____

        Manufacturer _____

        Retailer _____

        Date _____ Cost/unit $ _____

        No. of units _____ Total cost $ _____

        R-value added _____ Previous R-value _____

        Aggregate R-value _____ Thickness _____

        Type of vapor barrier *(6 mil poly, etc.)* _____

        Installed by _____

        Date _____ Cost $ _____

OTHER INSULATION • Insulation

_____

_____

_____

_____

_____

_____

_____

_____

INSULATION

Notes

Notes

> *What's the good of a home if you are never in it?*
>
> —George Grossmith

FIXTURES

Notes

FIXTURES

Room	Item	Brand

Retailer	Date	Cost	Warranty

Notes

Tip: Install dimmer switches for your light fixtures. This not only gives you more options, but is also a money saver!

105

PLUMBING

PLUMBING

Notes

106

Notes

Tip: Use cardboard under your furniture when moving it, and it will slide more easily.

BASEMENT/
ATTIC

Notes

BASEMENT/ATTIC

108

MISCELLANEOUS ITEMS

Door Chimes

Intercom System

Security System

Sewer/Septic System

Smoke/Fire Detector

Sump Pump

Thermostats

Water Heaters

Water Softener

Well

Whirlpool/Hot Tub/Sauna

Whole House Vacuum

Notes

▶ **Tip:** Venting: You should have one square foot of free-flowing cross-ventilation for every 150 square feet of floor space in the attic. Soffit vents with screen covers can reduce airflow by up to 75 percent.

EXTERIOR

ROOF

MEASUREMENTS • Roof
Width _____ X Depth _____ = _____ sq. ft.

TYPE & MATERIAL • Roof
Description *(fiberglass shingles, cedar shakes, etc.)* _____
Brand & style _____
Color & number _____
Misc. materials _____ Cost $ _____

PURCHASE • Roof
Retailer _____
Date _____ Cost/unit $ _____
No. of units _____ Total cost $ _____
Warranty _____

INSTALLATION • Roof
Installer _____
Date _____ Cost $ _____

MAINTENANCE • Roof
Company _____
  Date _____ Cost $ _____
Company _____
  Date _____ Cost $ _____

GUTTERS/DOWNSPOUTS

▶ **TYPE & MATERIAL** • Gutters
Description *(steel, vinyl, etc.)* _____
Brand & style _____
Color & number _____

PURCHASE • Gutters
Retailer _____
Date _____ Cost/unit $ _____
No. of units _____ Total cost $ _____
Warranty _____

INSTALLATION • Gutters
Installer _____
Date _____ Cost $ _____

Notes
_____
_____
_____
_____
_____
_____
_____
_____
_____
_____
_____
_____
_____
_____
_____
_____
_____
_____
_____
_____
_____
_____
_____
_____
_____
_____

Gutters/Downspouts *(continued)*

▶ **TYPE & MATERIAL** • Downspouts
　　Description *(steel, vinyl, etc.)* _____
　　Brand & style _____
　　Color & number _____

PURCHASE • Downspouts
　　Retailer _____
　　Date _____　　Cost/unit $ _____
　　No. of units _____　　Total cost $ _____
　　Warranty _____

INSTALLATION • Downspouts
　　Installer _____
　　Date _____　　Cost $ _____

SIDING

MEASUREMENTS • First Type of Siding
　　North: Width _____ X Height _____ = _____ sq. ft.
　　South: Width _____ X Height _____ = _____ sq. ft.
　　East:　 Width _____ X Height _____ = _____ sq. ft.
　　West:　Width _____ X Height _____ = _____ sq. ft.

▶ **TYPE & MATERIAL** • First Type of Siding
　　Description *(brick, stucco, etc.)* _____
　　　　Brand & style _____
　　　　Color & number _____
　　Type of finish *(paint, stain, etc.)* _____
　　　　Brand & number _____
　　　　Color & finish _____

PURCHASE • First Type of Siding
　　Retailer _____
　　Date _____　　Cost/unit $ _____
　　No. of units _____　　Total cost $ _____
　　Warranty _____

INSTALLATION • First Type of Siding
　　Installer _____
　　Date _____　　Cost $ _____

CLEANING & REFINISHING • First Type of Siding
　　Company _____
　　　　Date _____　　Cost $ _____
　　Company _____
　　　　Date _____　　Cost $ _____

Notes

_____
_____
_____
_____
_____
_____
_____
_____
_____
_____
_____
_____
_____
_____
_____
_____
_____
_____
_____

▶ **Tip:** Invest in the best materials you can afford. Quality is always worth the price.

✏️ *Notes*

MEASUREMENTS • Second Type of Siding

North: Width _____ X Height _____ = _____ sq. ft.

South: Width _____ X Height _____ = _____ sq. ft.

East: Width _____ X Height _____ = _____ sq. ft.

West: Width _____ X Height _____ = _____ sq. ft.

▶ **TYPE & MATERIAL** • Second Type of Siding

Description *(brick, stucco, etc.)* _____

Brand & style _____

Color & number _____

Type of finish *(paint, stain, etc.)* _____

Brand & number _____

Color & finish _____

PURCHASE • Second Type of Siding

Retailer _____

Date _____ Cost/unit $ _____

No. of units _____ Total cost $ _____

Warranty _____

INSTALLATION • Second Type of Siding

Installer _____

Date _____ Cost $ _____

CLEANING & REFINISHING • Second Type of Siding

Company _____

Date _____ Cost $ _____

Company _____

Date _____ Cost $ _____

TRIM

▶ **TYPE & MATERIAL** • First Type of Trim

Description *(wood, vinyl, etc.)* _____

Brand & style _____

Color & number _____

Type of finish *(paint, stain, etc.)* _____

Brand & number _____

Color & finish _____

PURCHASE • First Type of Trim

Retailer _____

Date _____ Cost/unit $ _____

No. of units _____ Total cost $ _____

Warranty _____

Trim *(continued)*

INSTALLATION • First Type of Trim
Installer _____
Date _____ Cost $ _____

CLEANING & REFINISHING • First Type of Trim
Company _____
   Date _____ Cost $ _____
Company _____
   Date _____ Cost $ _____

▶ **TYPE & MATERIAL** • Second Type of Trim
Description *(wood, vinyl, etc.)* _____
   Brand & style _____
   Color & number _____
Type of finish *(paint, stain, etc.)* _____
   Brand & number _____
   Color & finish _____

PURCHASE • Second Type of Trim
Retailer _____
Date _____ Cost/unit $ _____
No. of units _____ Total cost $ _____
Warranty _____

INSTALLATION • Second Type of Trim
Installer _____
Date _____ Cost $ _____

CLEANING & REFINISHING • Second Type of Trim
Company _____
   Date _____ Cost $ _____
Company _____
   Date _____ Cost $ _____

STORM WINDOWS

TYPE & MATERIAL • Storm Windows
Description *(wood, vinyl, etc.)* _____
   Brand & style _____
   Color & number _____
Type of finish *(paint, stain, etc.)* _____
   Brand & number _____
   Color & finish _____

PURCHASE • Storm Windows
Retailer _____
Date _____ Cost/unit $ _____

Notes

_____
_____
_____
_____
_____
_____
_____
_____
_____
_____
_____
_____
_____
_____
_____
_____
_____
_____
_____

A house is a home when it shelters the body and comforts the soul.

—Phillip Moffitt

EXTERIOR

Notes

_____
_____
_____
_____
_____
_____
_____
_____
_____
_____
_____
_____
_____
_____
_____
_____
_____
_____
_____
_____
_____
_____
_____
_____
_____

Storm Windows *(continued)*

No. of units _____ Total cost $ _____
  Warranty _____

INSTALLATION • Storm Windows
  Installer _____
  Date _____ Cost $ _____

CLEANING & REFINISHING • Storm Windows
  Company _____
  Date _____ Cost $ _____

STORM DOORS

MEASUREMENTS • Storm Doors
  First Storm Door: Second Storm Door:
  Width ____ Height ____   Width ____ Height ____

▶ **TYPE & MATERIAL** • First Storm Door
  Description *(wood, vinyl, etc.)* _____
  Brand & style _____
  Color & number _____
  Hardware description _____

PURCHASE • First Storm Door
  Retailer _____
  Date _____ Cost/unit $ _____
  No. of units _____ Total cost $ _____
  Warranty _____

INSTALLATION • First Storm Door
  Installer _____
  Date _____ Cost $ _____

▶ **TYPE & MATERIAL** • Second Storm Door
  Description *(wood, vinyl, etc.)* _____
  Brand & style _____
  Color & number _____
  Hardware description _____

PURCHASE • Second Storm Door
  Retailer _____
  Date _____ Cost/unit $ _____
  No. of units _____ Total cost $ _____
  Warranty _____

INSTALLATION • Second Storm Door
  Installer _____
  Date _____ Cost $ _____

DECK

MEASUREMENTS • Deck

Width _____ X Depth _____ = _____ sq. ft.

TYPE & MATERIAL • Deck

Description *(redwood, green treated, etc.)* _____
    Brand & number _____
Type of finish/sealer *(paint, stain, etc.)* _____
    Brand & number _____
    Color & finish _____

PURCHASE • Deck

Retailer _____
Date _____ Cost/unit $ _____
No. of units _____ Total cost $ _____
Warranty _____

INSTALLATION • Deck

Installer _____
Date _____ Cost $ _____

CLEANING & REFINISHING • Deck

Company _____
    Date _____ Cost $ _____
Company _____
    Date _____ Cost $ _____

PATIO

MEASUREMENTS • Patio

Width _____ X Depth _____ = _____ sq. ft.

TYPE & MATERIAL • Patio

Description *(patio blocks, cement, etc.)* _____
Brand & style _____
Color & number _____
Misc. materials _____ Cost $ _____

PURCHASE • Patio

Retailer _____
Date _____ Cost/unit $ _____
No. of units _____ Total cost $ _____
Warranty _____

INSTALLATION • Patio

Installer _____
Date _____ Cost $ _____

Notes

_____

Tip: Keep plants far enough away from your house, deck or patio that you can walk between the plants and the structure. Plants that are too close can cause dampness, which will promote wood rot and bug infestations.

115

Patio *(continued)*

MAINTENANCE • Patio
 Company
  Date   Cost $

DRIVEWAY

MEASUREMENTS • Driveway
 Width   X Depth   =   sq. ft.

TYPE & MATERIAL • Driveway
 Description *(asphalt, concrete, etc.)*
 Brand & style
 Color & number

PURCHASE • Driveway
 Retailer
 Date   Cost/unit $
 No. of units   Total cost $
 Warranty

INSTALLATION • Driveway
 Installer
 Date   Cost $

MAINTENANCE • Driveway
 Company
  Date   Cost $

FENCES

▶ **MEASUREMENTS** • Fence 1
 Height   Linear feet

TYPE & MATERIAL • Fence 1
 Description *(cedar, chain link, etc.)*
  Brand & number
 Type of finish/sealer *(paint, stain, etc.)*
  Brand & number
  Color & finish

PURCHASE • Fence 1
 Retailer
 Date   Cost/unit $
 No. of units   Total cost $
 Warranty

Fences *(continued)*

INSTALLATION • Fence 1
    Installer
    Date   Cost $

MAINTENANCE • Fence 1
    Company
        Date   Cost $

▶ **MEASUREMENTS** • Fence 2
    Height   Linear feet

TYPE & MATERIAL • Fence 2
    Description *(cedar, chain link, etc.)*
        Brand & number
    Type of finish/sealer *(paint, stain, etc.)*
        Brand & number
        Color & finish

PURCHASE • Fence 2
    Retailer
    Date   Cost/unit $
    No. of units   Total cost $
    Warranty

INSTALLATION • Fence 2
    Installer
    Date   Cost $

MAINTENANCE • Fence 2
    Company
        Date   Cost $

GAZEBO

PURCHASE • Gazebo
    Retailer
    Date   Cost/unit $
    No. of units   Total cost $
    Warranty

INSTALLATION • Gazebo
    Installer
    Date   Cost $

MAINTENANCE • Gazebo
    Company
        Date   Cost $

Notes

HOW TO

FURNACE TUNE-UP CHECKLIST
- Inspect thermostat
- Inspect filter: change/clean
- Check all electricals
- Oil motors
- Inspect heat exchanger for cracks
- Check air flow: clean coil if necessary
- Check air/fuel mixture where appropriate

EXTERIOR

Notes

PORCH

OUTBUILDINGS

118

LAWN&GARDEN

OUTDOOR DIARY

Record special events or occurrences around your lawn and garden, such as the earliest you've sighted a robin, when you picked that first tomato of the season, or notable climate characteristics.

1st/earliest _____

1st/earliest _____

Last _____

Last _____

Most rain _____

Heat wave/highest temp _____

Cold wave/coldest temp _____

Last snow/most snow _____

Earliest fall frost _____

Latest spring frost _____

Growing season _____

Record vegetable size or harvest _____

Bird sightings _____

Wildlife sightings _____

Other _____

Notes

Plant more trees to give the world more oxygen.

—Joshua, age 6

LAWN & GARDEN

TREES/SHRUBS/PERENNIALS

Plant Type	Size	Quantity

Retailer	Date	Cost	Care Instructions

Notes

Tip: Safety first! Before you begin an outside project that requires digging in your yard, always call the utility companies to find out where gas lines and cables are buried.

LAWN & GARDEN

_____

_____

✏️ Notes
_____
_____
_____
_____
_____
_____
_____
_____
_____
_____
_____
_____
_____
_____
_____
_____
_____
_____
_____
_____
_____
_____
_____
_____
_____
_____

EQUIPMENT

▶ **TYPE** • Equipment 1
  Description _(tractor, mower, etc.)_
  Brand
  Model   Serial no.

  PURCHASE • Equipment 1
  Retailer
  Date   Cost $
  Warranty

  MAINTENANCE & SERVICE • Equipment 1
  Company
    Date   Cost $
  Company
    Date   Cost $

▶ **TYPE** • Equipment 2
  Description _(tractor, mower, etc.)_
  Brand
  Model   Serial no.

  PURCHASE • Equipment 2
  Retailer
  Date   Cost $
  Warranty

  MAINTENANCE & SERVICE • Equipment 2
  Company
    Date   Cost $
  Company
    Date   Cost $

▶ **TYPE** • Equipment 3
  Description _(tractor, mower, etc.)_
  Brand
  Model   Serial no.

  PURCHASE • Equipment 3
  Retailer
  Date   Cost $
  Warranty

  MAINTENANCE & SERVICE • Equipment 3
  Company
    Date   Cost $
  Company
    Date   Cost $

SWIMMING POOL

Notes

Tip: Plants thrive
in fertile soil. Make
sure your garden
soil is rich in nutri-
ents for the best
results, no matter what you
are growing. Many plant
foods are available for spe-
cific types of plants, but
they all work best in conjunction with a solid base
of nutrient-rich soil.

LAWN & GARDEN

Notes

Arbor/Trellis/Lattice

Barbeque/Grill

Bird Feeders & Baths

Compost Bin

Furniture, Outdoor

Glider & Swing, Outdoor

Lighting, Outdoor

Play Area & Swing Set

Retaining Walls

Sprinkler System

Statues & Ornaments

GARDEN/YARD DIAGRAMS

Notes

Tip: Plan for ample storage—nobody ever has enough.

LAWN & GARDEN

Notes

GARDEN/YARD DIAGRAMS

GARDEN/YARD DIAGRAMS

Notes

> *You've become as exciting as your foodblender. The kids come in, look you in the eye, and ask if anybody's home.*
>
> —Erma Bombeck

FINANCE&INSURANCE

Notes
_____
_____
_____
_____
_____
_____
_____
_____
_____
_____
_____
_____
_____
_____
_____
_____
_____
_____
_____
_____
_____
_____
_____
_____
_____
_____
_____
_____
_____
_____
_____

PURCHASE

Closing Date _____
Purchase Price $ _____
Occupancy Date _____
Square Footage of Home _____
Legal Description of Property _____
_____
_____
_____

Contacts:	Company	Contact	Phone
Builder			
Land Developer			
Realtor			
Title Company			

Construction Warranty _____
_____
_____
_____
_____

Lot Marker Locations _____
_____
_____
_____
_____

FINANCE

Mortgage Company _____
    Phone _____
Loan Officer _____
    Phone _____
Loan Number _____

Finance *(continued)*

Mortgage Amount $ _____

Mortgage Type *(FHA, VA, conventional, etc)* _____

Interest Rate _____

Terms *(fixed, adjustable etc.)* _____

Amortization Period *(30 year, 15 year, etc.)* _____

Points *(percent & dollar amount)* _____

New Mortgage Company _____

    Phone _____

Loan Number _____

Date Mortgage Sold _____

INSURANCE

Title Insurance Company _____

    Phone _____

    Policy Number _____

Homeowner's Insurance Company _____

    Phone _____

    Agent _____

    Agent Phone _____

    Policy Number _____

    Expiration Date _____

Notes

▶ **Tip:** Remember tax effects. Permanent renovations, such as room additions, new cabinets, and doors, increase the tax value of your home.

TAX EFFECTS
OF IMPROVING AND REPAIRING YOUR HOME

Y ou could be subject to income taxes when you sell your home. The amount of these income taxes will be based, in part, on the difference between the sales price of your home and its *tax basis*. The *tax basis* is computed by adding the cost of the various improvements that you make to your home to the original purchase price. It is important, therefore, that you generally understand that improvements increase the *basis*, and that ongoing repairs do not.

Improvements to your home generally include more permanent items such as finishing the basement, room additions, new storm windows, roof replacement, new deck, and landscaping, fencing and swimming pool installation. The Internal Revenue Service permits improvements to be added to the *basis* of a home, provided that the homeowner has kept adequate records, such as invoices, date and cost, of the improvements. If you've paid a contractor to improve your home, the contractor's fees are included in the *tax basis*, provided you have adequate records of the fees. *The Home Owner's Journal* can store these records, for both the materials and the contractor's labor, of a home improvement. You can, for example, write the description, date and cost of an improvement in the appropriate section of this book and you may store the corresponding invoice(s) in the pocket page in the back of the book.

Repairs, however, are not included in the *tax basis* of your home, unless you perform the repairs in conjunction with the larger renovation of your home. Repairs include items such as repainting, driveway recoating, window repair, furnace repair and electrical fixture replacement.

The IRS offers instruction for determining the tax effects of improving and repairing your home in IRS Publication 523, *Selling Your Home*. You may obtain a free copy of Publication 523 at the IRS's website, www.irs.gov . Alternatively, you may consult with a qualified tax professional.

INDEX

131